A Text Book Of

DATA WAREHOUSING WITH MINING TECHNIQUES

(22621)

Semester - VI

THIRD YEAR DIPLOMA IN COMPUTER ENGINEERING GROUP

As Per MSBTE's 'I' Scheme Syllabus

Dr. Meenakshi A. Thalor
Ph.D. (Computer Engineering), M.E. (I.T.), B. Tech. (I.T.)
Head of Department & Associate Professor, Information Technology
AISSMS Institute of Information Technology
Pune

Prashant D. Somwanshi
M.E. (Computer Engineering)
Lecturer, Dept. of Computer Engineering
JSPM & TSSM Group of Institutes
Bhivarabai Sawant College of Engineering & Research Polytechnic
Narhe, Pune

NIRALI PRAKASHAN
ADVANCEMENT OF KNOWLEDGE

N4400

Data Warehousing with Mining Techniques **ISBN : 978-93-89825-18-3**

First Edition : **December 2019**

Published By :

NIRALI PRAKASHAN

Abhyudaya Pragati, 1312, Shivaji Nagar

Off J.M. Road, PUNE – 411005

Tel - (020) 25512336/37/39, Fax - (020) 25511379

Email : niralipune@pragationline.com

➢ DISTRIBUTION CENTRES

PUNE

Nirali Prakashan (For orders within Pune) : 119, Budhwar Peth, Jogeshwari Mandir Lane, Pune 411002, Maharashtra
Tel : (020) 2445 2044, 66022708, Fax : (020) 2445 1538; Mobile : 9657703145
Email : niralilocal@pragationline.com

Nirali Prakashan (For orders outside Pune) : S. No. 28/27, Dhayari, Near Asian College Pune 411041
Tel : (020) 24690204 Fax : (020) 24690316; Mobile : 9657703143
Email : bookorder@pragationline.com

MUMBAI

Nirali Prakashan : 385, S.V.P. Road, Rasdhara Co-op. Hsg. Society Ltd.,
Girgaum, Mumbai 400004, Maharashtra; Mobile : 9320129587
Tel : (022) 2385 6339 / 2386 9976, Fax : (022) 2386 9976
Email : niralimumbai@pragationline.com

➢ DISTRIBUTION BRANCHES

JALGAON

Nirali Prakashan : 34, V. V. Golani Market, Navi Peth, Jalgaon 425001, Maharashtra,
Tel : (0257) 222 0395, Mob : 94234 91860; Email : niralijalgaon@pragationline.com

KOLHAPUR

Nirali Prakashan : New Mahadvar Road, Kedar Plaza, 1st Floor Opp. IDBI Bank, Kolhapur 416 012
Maharashtra. Mob : 9850046155; Email : niralikolhapur@pragationline.com

NAGPUR

Nirali Prakashan : Above Maratha Mandir, Shop No. 3, First Floor,
Rani Jhanshi Square, Sitabuldi, Nagpur 440012, Maharashtra
Tel : (0712) 254 7129; Email : niralinagpur@pragationline.com

DELHI

Nirali Prakashan : 4593/15, Basement, Agarwal Lane, Ansari Road, Daryaganj
Near Times of India Building, New Delhi 110002 Mob : 08505972553
Email : niralidelhi@pragationline.com

BENGALURU

Nirali Prakashan : Maitri Ground Floor, Jaya Apartments, No. 99, 6th Cross, 6th Main,
Malleswaram, Bengaluru 560003, Karnataka; Mob : 9449043034
Email: niralibangalore@pragationline.com

Other Branches : Hyderabad, Chennai

niralipune@pragationline.com | www.pragationline.com

Also find us on f www.facebook.com/niralibooks

Preface ...

We take an opportunity to present this book entitled as "**Data Warehousing with Mining Techniques**" to the students of Sixth Semester (Third Year Diploma in Computer Engineering). The object of this book is to present the subject matter in a most concise and simple manner. The book is written strictly according to the Revised Syllabus (I-Scheme) prepared by Maharashtra State Board of Technical Education (MSBTE).

This book contains Five constructive chapters.

- First chapter gives introduction to data warehousing.
- Second chapter focusses on data warehouse modeling and online analytical processing I.
- Third chapter covers data warehouse designing and online analytical processing II.
- Fourth chapter introduces concepts of data mining.
- Mining frequent patterns and cluster analysis are covered in fifth chapter.

A special words of thank to Shri. Dineshbhai Furia, Mr. Jignesh Furia for showing full faith in us to write this text book. We also thank to Mr. Amar Salunkhe, Mrs. Yojana Deshpande and Mrs. Surekha Sannali of M/s Nirali Prakashan for their excellent co-operation.

We also thank Mr. Ravindra Walodare, Mr. Sachin Shinde, Mr. Ashok Bodke, Mr. Moshin Sayyed and Mr. Nitin Thorat.

We welcome constructive suggestions from our colleagues and students.

Authors

Syllabus ...

1. Introduction to Data Warehousing

1.1 Data Warehousing, Difference between Operational Database System and Data Warehouse.

1.2 Need for Data Warehousing

1.3 A Multi-tiered Architecture of Data Warehousing.

1.4 Data Warehouse Models : Enterprise Warehouse, Data Mart, and Virtual Warehouse.

1.5 Extraction, Transformation and Loading.

.1.6 Metadata Repository.

1.7 Benefits of Data Warehousing.

2. Warehouse Modeling and Online Analytical Processing I

2.1 Data Warehouse Modeling: Data Cube and OLAP, Data Cube: A Multi-dimensional Data Model.

2.2 Stars, Snowflakes and Fact Constellations.

2.3 OLAP: Need of OLAP, OLAP Guidelines.

2.4 Typical OLAP Operations.

3. Warehouse Designing and Online Analytical Processing II

3.1 Data Warehouse Design and Usage.

3.2 A Business Analysis Framework for Data Warehouse Design.

3.3 Data Warehouse Design Process.

3.4 Data Warehouse Usage for Information Processing. From Online Analytical Processing to Multi-dimensional Data Mining.

3.5 Data Warehouse Implementation Efficient Data Cube Computation: An Overview.

3.6 Indexing OLAP Data : Bitmap Index and Join Index, Efficient Processing of OLAP Queries.

3.7 OLAP Server Architectures: ROLAP versus MOLAP versus HOLAP

4. Introduction to Data Mining

4.1 Introduction to Data Mining: Mining Steps in the Process of Knowledge Discovery of Database (KDD).

4.2 What Kind of Data can be Mined? Major Issues in Data Mining.

4.3 Data Objects and Attributes Types.

4.4 Data Preprocessing: Why Preprocess the Data? Major Tasks in Data Preprocessing.

4.5 Data Cleaning: Missing Values, Noisy Data, Data Cleaning as a Process.

5. Mining Frequent Patterns and Cluster Analysis

5.1 Mining Frequent Patterns: Basic Concepts, Market Basket Analysis, Frequent Itemsets, Closed Itemsets, and Association Rules.

5.2 Frequent Itemsets Mining Methods: The Apriori Algorithm, Finding Frequent Itemsets Using Candidate Generation.

5.3 Generating Association Rules from Frequent Itemsets.

5.4 What is Cluster Analysis?

5.5 Overview of Basic Clustering Methods.

5.6 General Applications of Clustering.

❖ ❖ ❖

Contents ...

1. Introduction to Data Warehousing **1.1 – 1.22**

1.0 Introduction 1.1
1.1 Data Warehouse and Data Warehousing 1.2
1.1.1 Data Warehouse 1.2
1.1.2 Data Warehousing 1.2
1.1.3 Characteristics of Data Warehouse 1.3
1.1.4 Difference between Operational Database System and Data Warehouse 1.3
1.1.5 Components of Data Warehouse 1.4
1.2 Need for Data Warehousing 1.7
1.3 A multitier architecture of data warehousing 1.7
1.3.1 Single Layer Architecture of Data Warehouse 1.8
1.3.2 Two Layer Architecture of Data Warehouse 1.8
1.3.3 Three Tier Data Warehouse Architecture 1.9
1.4 Data Warehouse Model 1.10
1.4.1 Virtual Data Warehouse 1.11
1.4.2 Data Mart 1.12
1.4.3 Enterprise Data Warehouse 1.14
1.5 Extraction, Transformation and Loading (ETL) 1.14
1.6 Metadata Repository 1.18
1.7 Benefits of Data Warehousing 1.20
❖ Practice Questions 1.22

2. Warehouse Modeling and Online Analytical Processing I **2.1 – 2.14**

2.0 Introduction 2.1
2.1 Data Warehouse Modeling 2.1
2.1.1 Data Cube and OLAP 2.2
2.1.2 Data Cube 2.3
2.2 A Multidimensional Data Model 2.5
2.2.1 Star Schemas for Multidimensional Model 2.6
2.2.2 Snowflake Schemas for Multidimensional Model 2.6
2.2.3 Fact Constellation Schemas for Multidimensional Model 2.7
2.3 OLAP 2.8
2.3.1 Need of OLAP 2.8
2.3.2 OLAP Guidelines 2.9
2.4 Typical OLAP Operations 2.11
❖ Practice Questions 2.14

3. Warehouse Designing and Online Analytical Processing II **3.1 – 3.22**

3.0 Introduction 3.1
3.1 Data Warehouse Design And Usage 3.2
3.1.1 Data Warehouse Design 3.2
3.1.2 Usage of Data Warehouse 3.4
3.2 A Business Analysis Framework For Data Warehouse Design 3.6
3.3 Data Warehouse Design Process 3.7

3.4	Data Warehouse Useage For Information Processing	3.9
	3.4.1 From OLAP to Multidimensional Data Mining	3.10
3.5	Data Warehouse Implementation	3.11
	3.5.1 Efficient Data Cube Computation (An Overview)	3.11
3.6	Indexing OLAP data (Bitmap index and join index)	3.14
	3.6.1 Bitmap Indexing	3.14
	3.6.2 Joint Indexing	3.15
	3.6.3 Efficient Processing of OLAP Queries	3.17
3.7	OLAP Server Architecture	3.18
	3.7.1 MOLAP Model	3.19
	3.7.2 ROLAP Model	3.20
	3.7.3 HOLAP Model	3.21
❖	Practice Questions	3.22
4.	**Introduction to Data Mining**	**4.1 – 4.30**
4.0	Introduction	4.1
4.1	Introduction to Data Mining	4.2
	4.1.1 Mining Steps in Process of KDD	4.4
	4.1.2 Data Mining Tasks	4.7
4.2	What Type of Data can be Mined?	4.9
	4.2.1 Issues in Data Mining	4.11
4.3	Data Objects And Attributes	4.12
4.4	Data Preprocessing	4.15
	4.4.1 Why Preprocess the Data?	4.15
	4.4.2 Major Task in Preprocessing	4.16
4.5	Data Cleaning	4.24
	4.5.1 Data Cleaning as a Process	4.26
	4.5.2 Data Mining Technology and its Relation to Data Warehousing	4.28
❖	Practice Questions	4.30
5.	**Mining Frequent Patterns and Cluster Analysis**	**5.1 – 5.20**
5.0	Introduction	5.1
5.1	Mining Frequent Pattern (Basic concept)	5.2
	5.1.1 Market Basket Analysis	5.3
	5.1.2 Frequent Itemset, Closed Itemset and Association Rules	5.5
5.2	Frequent Itemset Mining Methods	5.8
	5.2.1 Apriori Algorithm (Finding Frequent Itemset using Candidate Generation)	5.8
5.3	Generating Association Rules from Frequent Itemsets	5.12
5.4	What Is Cluster Analysis?	5.13
	5.4.1 Requirement of Cluster Analysis	5,15
5.5	Overview of Basic Clustering Methods	5.16
5.6	General Applications of Clustering	5.20
❖	Practice Questions	5.20

❖ ❖ ❖

1...

Introduction to Data Warehousing

Chapter Outcomes...

- Describe need and architecture for the given data warehouse.
- Explain the benefits of data warehousing of the given application.
- Describe the given data warehouse models.
- Describe Extraction, Transformation and Loading (ETL) for the given data warehouse.
- Describe metadata repository for the given data warehouse.

Learning Objectives...

- To understand Basic Concepts in Data Warehouse and Data Warehousing
- To learn Architecture of Data Warehousing
- To study various Data Warehouse Models (Data Mart, Virtual Warehouse etc.)
- To understand ETL Concept in Data Warehouse
- To know Benefits of Data Warehousing

1.0 INTRODUCTION

- The task of getting any meaningful data or information out of the early computer systems used to be very complex and tedious. Consequently, a number of methods, techniques and tools were developed to solve that problem.
- These included decentralized processing, extract processing, Executive, Information Systems (EIS), query tools, relational databases, etc. The need for timely and accurate decisions also led to the development of Decision Support Systems (DSSs).
- Data warehousing began to grow explosively starting in the mid-nineties. It is still characterized by high growth.
- Data warehousing is the process of constructing and using a data warehouse. Data warehousing is the process of constructing and using a data warehouse. The data warehouse is a basis for informational processing.
- Data warehousing enables easy organization and maintenance of large data in addition to fast retrieval and analysis in the manner and depth required from time to time.
- Data Warehousing, OnLine Analytical Processing (OLAP) and Data Mining represent some of the latest trends in computing environment and Information Technology (IT) applications to large-scale processing and analysis of data.

- Data mining is the process of discovering new information out of data in a data warehouse, which cannot be retrieved within the operational system.
- Data mining refers to the extraction of useful information from a bulk of data or data warehouses. Data mining is the computational process of discovering patterns in large data sets involving methods at the intersection of artificial intelligence, machine learning, statistics, and database systems.

1.1 DATA WAREHOUSE AND DATA WAREHOUSING

- Data warehousing is the process of constructing and using a data warehouse. A data warehouse is constructed by integrating data from multiple heterogeneous sources that support analytical reporting, structured and/or ad hoc queries, and decision making.
- Data warehousing involves data cleaning, data integration, and data consolidations.

1.1.1 Data Warehouse

- A database contains information organized in columns, rows and tables that is periodically indexed to make accessing relevant information more accessible.
- Many enterprises and organizations create and manage databases using a database management system. Special DBMS software can be used create and store product inventory and customer information. Organizations most often use databases for OnLine Transaction Processing (OLTP).
- A database was built to store current transactions and enable fast access to specific transactions for ongoing business processes, known as OnLine Transaction Processing (OLTP).
- Most enterprises generate unlimited amounts of data from their OLTP systems, Point-of-Service (PoS) systems, financial ATMs and the Web.
- The challenge faced by these enterprises/organizations with regard to the massive data-rich but information-poor collection is to extract valuable information to be available at a particular time, place and in the form needed to support the decision-making process.
- The term "data warehouse" was first coined by Bill Inmon in 1990. According to Inmon, a data warehouse is a subject oriented, integrated, time-variant, and non-volatile collection of data. This data helps analysts to take informed decisions in an organization.
- A Data Warehouse (DW) is a collection of technologies aimed at enabling the knowledge worker (executive, manager, and analyst) to make better and faster decisions.
- It is expected to have the right information in the right place at the right time with the right cost in order to support the right decision.
- Data warehouses and databases are both relational data systems, but were built to serve different purposes. A data warehouse is built to store large quantities of historical data and enable fast, complex queries across all the data, typically using OnLine Analytical Processing (OLAP).

1.1.2 Data Warehousing

- A data warehouse is a database, which is kept separate from the organization's operational database. A data warehouse is a collection of data specific to the entire organization.
- A data warehouse is a decision-support environment that leverages data stored in different sources, organizing it and delivering it to decision makers across the enterprise, regardless of their platform or technical skill level.

- In short, a data warehouse is a database designed to support decision making in an organization.
- Data warehouse systems are currently well established within several medium to large organizations and it is widely acknowledged that they play a strategic role when it comes to providing end users with easy access to key information that would otherwise be hardly available.
- A data warehouse can provide a central repository for large amounts of historical, integrated, and consistent data.
- By filing the data into a central point of storage, the data warehouse provides an integrated representation of the multiple sources of information dispatch across the enterprise.
- Data warehouse is equipped with tools that offer company/organization management the opportunity to extract reliable information to be used as a support for a decision-making process.
- Data warehousing involves processes that extract relevant data from an enterprise information system, transform the data, integrate it, remove any flaws and inconsistencies, store it into a data warehouse, and provide end users with access to the data so that they can carry out complex data analysis and prediction queries.
- A data warehouse ensures the consistency of management rules and conventions applied to the data.
- It also provides the appropriate tools to extract specific data, convert it into business information, and monitor for changes and hence, it is possible to use this information to make insightful decisions.

1.1.3 Characteristics of Data Warehouse

- The formal definition of a data warehouse by W. H. Inmon is given below:

  "A data warehouse is a subject-oriented, integrated, time-varying, non-volatile collection of data in support of the management's decision-making process."
- The key **characteristics/features of a data warehouse** are discussed below:
  1. **Subject Oriented:** A data warehouse is subject oriented because it provides information around a subject rather than the organization's ongoing operations. These subjects can be product, customers, suppliers, sales, revenue, etc. A data warehouse does not focus on the ongoing operations, rather it focuses on modelling and analysis of data for decision making.
  2. **Integrated:** A data warehouse is constructed by integrating data from heterogeneous sources such as relational databases, flat files, etc. This integration enhances the effective analysis of data.
  3. **Time Variant:** The data collected in a data warehouse is identified with a particular time period. The data in a data warehouse provides information from the historical point of view.
  4. **Non-volatile:** Non-volatile means the previous data is not erased when new data is added to it. A data warehouse is always a physically separated store of data. Due to this separation, data warehouse does not require transaction processing, recovery, concurrency control, etc.
- A data warehouse is kept separate from the operational database and therefore frequent changes in operational database is not reflected in the data warehouse.

1.1.4 Difference between Operational Database System and Data Warehouse

- Operational database management systems also called as OLTP (OnLine Transactions Processing Databases), are used to manage dynamic data in real-time. Following table shows the differences between OLTP and data warehouse.

Sr. No.	Operational Database System	Data Warehouse
1.	Operational database systems are designed to support high-volume transaction processing.	Data warehousing systems are typically designed to support high-volume analytical processing (i.e., OLAP).
2.	Operational database systems are usually concerned with current data.	Data warehousing systems are usually concerned with historical data.
3.	Data within operational systems are mainly updated regularly according to need.	Non-volatile, new data may be added regularly. Once, the data added rarely changed.
4.	It is designed for real-time business dealing and processes.	It is designed for analysis of business measures by subject area, categories, and attributes.
5.	It is optimized for a simple set of transactions, generally adding or retrieving a single row at a time per table.	It is optimized for extent loads and high, complex, unpredictable queries that access many rows per table.
6.	It is optimized for validation of incoming information during transactions, uses validation data tables.	Loaded with consistent, valid information, requires no real-time validation.
7.	It supports thousands of concurrent clients.	It supports a few concurrent clients relative to OLTP.
8.	Operational database systems are widely functional or process-oriented.	Data warehousing systems are widely subject-oriented.
9.	Operational systems are usually optimized to perform fast inserts and updates of associatively small volumes of data.	Data warehousing systems are usually optimized to perform fast retrievals of relatively high volumes of data.
10.	Operational database system focuses on Data In	Data warehousing system focuses on Data Out
11.	Less number of data accessed.	Large number of data accessed.
12.	Relational databases are created for OLTP.	Data warehouse designed for OLAP.
13.	Data integration in operational database is application based.	Data integration data warehouse is subject based.
14.	It provides detailed and flat relational view of data.	It provides summarized and multidimensional view of data.

1.1.5 Components of Data Warehouse

- A data warehouse consists of various components (building blocks) which are arranged in the most optimum way to get the maximum benefit out of it.
- The arrangement of these components mainly depends on certain circumstances and information requirements of an organization.

- However, whether a data warehouse is being built for a larger organization or for the smaller one, the basic components remain the same; the only difference seen is in their arrangement. The basic components which comprise a typical data warehouse is shown in Fig. 1.1.

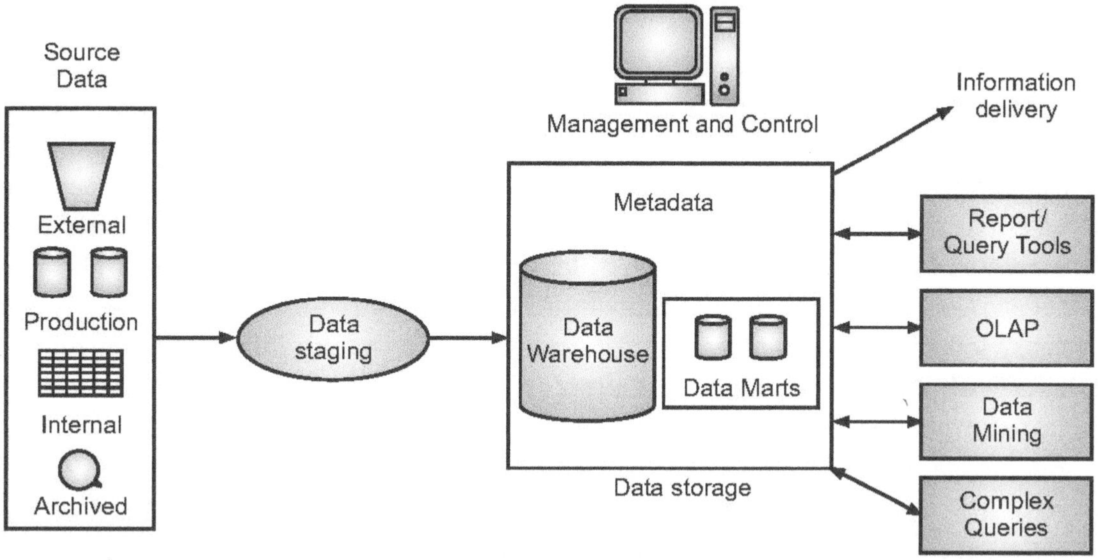

Fig. 1.1: Components of Data Warehouse

- The basic components of a data warehouse are explained below:
  1. **Source Data:** The source data comprises the data coming into the data warehouse from different areas. This source data can be grouped into following four categories:
     - **(i) Production Data:** The data in this category comprise different segments of data chosen from the various operational systems of the enterprise. The data are selected on the basis of requirements in data warehouse.
     - **(ii) Internal Data:** In every organization, users keep their personal data such as private spreadsheets, documents, customer profiles, departmental databases, etc. All these data form the internal data which could be useful in a data warehousing environment.
     - **(iii) Archived Data:** This is a compiled form of older data which is stored in archived files such as tape cartridges, flat files, etc. As data warehouse contains data of many years, so depending on the requirement, data warehouse data are archived from time to time.
     - **(iv) External Data:** It refers to those data sources which are available outside the organization. The production, internal and archived data give an insight view of what organization is doing presently and have done in the past. However, by including external data in data warehouse, executives can spot current trends availing in the market and can compare the performance of their organizations with others.
  2. **Data Staging Component:** After extracting data from various operational systems and external sources, data need to be prepared for storing in the data warehouse. The data staging component of data warehouse, helps in making data ready to be stored in data warehouse. It comprises following three main functions:
     - **(i) Data Extraction** function deals with a large amount of data sources and for each data source an appropriate technique must be applied. Data extraction is a complex and critical task, as source data may be from different source machines in various data formats and with different data models (relational, network or hierarchical). Various data extraction tools are available in the market today. The organization can use these tools for certain data sources. However, these tools incur high initial cost. For some other data sources, in-house

programs can also be developed. But, these may incur the development and maintenance cost. Generally, the data are extracted into a separate physical environment such as flat files, or a data-staging relational database from which moving the data into the data warehouse would be easier.

(ii) Data Transformation: The data sources may contain some minor errors or inconsistencies. For example, the names are often misspelled, and street, area or city names in the addresses are misspelled or zip codes are entered incorrectly. These incorrect data, thus, must be cleaned to minimize the errors and fill in the missing information when possible. The task of correcting and preprocessing the data is called data cleansing. These errors can he corrected to some reasonable level by looking up a database containing street names and zip codes in each city. The approximate matching of data required for this task is referred to as fuzzy lookup. In some cases, the data managers in the organization want to upgrade their data with the cleaned data. This process is known as back-flushing. These data are then transformed to accommodate semantic mismatches.

(iii) Data Loading: The cleaned and transformed data are finally loaded into the warehouse. Data are partitioned, and indexes or other access paths are built for fast and efficient retrieval of data. Loading is a slow process due to the large volume of data. For instance, loading a terabyte of data sequentially can take weeks and a gigabyte can take hours. Thus, parallelism is important for loading warehouses. The raw data generated by transaction-processing system may be too large to store in a data warehouse; therefore some data can be stored in a summarized form. Thus, additional preprocessing such as sorting and generation of summarized data is performed at this stage.

This entire process of getting data into the data warehouse is called Extract, Transform and Load (ETL) process. Once, the data is loaded into a warehouse, it must be periodically refreshed to reflect the updates on the relations at the data sources and periodically purge of old data.

3. **Data Storage Component:** This component consists of a separate repository for storing desired data in the data warehouse. In the data repository of a warehouse, huge amount of historical data are kept along with the current data in specific structures suitable for analysis; however, these repositories are made read-only in the data warehouse. This is because for analysis, one must not have data storage to be in such a state where continual updations are made to it.

4. **Information Delivery Component:** This component includes different methods for rendering information to the wide group of data warehouse users. Some common methods include ad hoc reports, Multi-Dimensional (MD) analysis, statistical analysis, Executive Information System (EIS) feed and data mining applications.

5. **Metadata Component:** Metadata is the data about the data. The metadata stores data in a similar way as the data dictionary or data catalogue does in a DBMS but it also keeps information about the logical data structures, files, addresses, indexes, etc.

6. **Management and Control Component:** This component of data warehouse manages and coordinates the various services and activities within the data warehouse from the beginning to the end. It also works with the database management system and enables data to be properly stored in the repositories. It controls the data transformation into the data warehouse storage and moderates information delivery to the users. It also supervises the movement of data into the staging area and from there into the data warehouse storage itself. While performing these functions, it interacts with the metadata component as metadata is the source of information for the management module.

1.2 NEED FOR DATA WAREHOUSING

- Data warehousing technology is becoming essential for effective business intelligence as it enables easy organization and maintenance of large data in addition to fast retrieval and analysis in the manner and depth required from time to time.
- Following points show the need and importance of data warehouse:
    1. Data warehouse helps business users to access critical data from some sources all in one place.
    2. It provides consistent information on various cross-functional activities.
    3. Data warehousing helps to integrate many sources of data to reduce stress on the production system.
    4. Data warehousing helps users to reduce total turnaround time for analysis and reporting.
    5. Data warehousing helps users to access critical data from different sources in a single place so, it saves user's time of retrieving data information from multiple sources. We can also access data from the cloud easily.
    6. Data warehousing allows to stores a large amount of historical data to analyze different periods and trends to make future predictions.
    7. Data warehousing enhances the value of operational business applications and customer relationship management systems.
    8. It separates analytics processing from transactional databases, improving the performance of both systems.
    9. Data warehousing provides more accurate reports.

1.3 A MULTI-TIERED ARCHITECTURE OF DATA WAREHOUSING

- Data warehousing provides architectures to systematically organize, understand, and use their data to make strategic decisions.
- Data warehouse architecture depends upon the organization's situation. The following **architecture properties** are essential for a data warehouse system:
    1. **Separation:** Analytical and transactional processing should be kept apart as much as possible.
    2. **Scalability:** Hardware and software architectures should be easy to upgrade as the data volume, which has to be managed and processed, and the number of users' requirements, which have to be met, progressively increase.
    3. **Extensibility:** The architecture should be able to host new applications and technologies without redesigning the whole system.
    4. **Security:** Monitoring accesses is essential because of the strategic data stored in data warehouses.
    5. **Administerability:** Data warehouse management should not be overly difficult.
- There are following three common types of data warehouse architectures:
    1. Basic architecture (single-layer) of data warehouse.
    2. Two layer architecture of data warehouse.
    3. Three layer architecture of data warehouse.

1.3.1 Single Layer Architecture of Data Warehouse

- Single layer architecture is a basic architecture of data warehouse which is not frequently used today. Single layer architecture is shown in Fig. 1.2.
- In single layer architecture, end users can access data directly from the various source systems through the data warehouse.
- The goal of basic architecture of data warehouse is to minimize the amount of data stored and remove the data redundancies.
- The basic structure lets end users of the warehouse directly access summary data derived from source systems and perform analysis, reporting, and mining on that data. This structure is useful for when data sources derive from the same types of database systems.

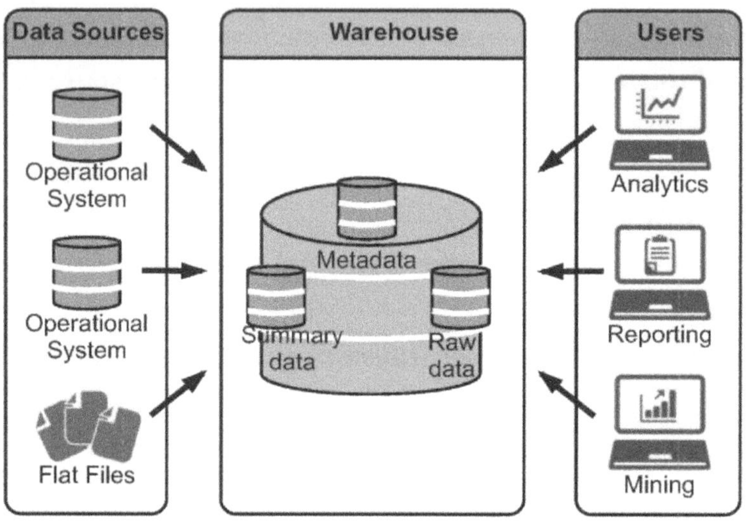

Fig. 1.2 : Basic Architecture of Data Warehouse

- The weakness of basic architecture of data warehouse architecture lies in its failure to meet the requirement for separation between analytical and transactional processing.
- Analysis queries are submitted to operational data after the middleware interprets them. It this way, the queries affect regular transactional workloads.
- In addition, although basic architecture of data warehouse architecture can meet the requirement for integration and correctness of data, it cannot log more data than sources do.
- For these reasons, a virtual approach to data warehouses can be successful only if analysis needs are particularly restricted and the data volume to analyze is huge.

1.3.2 Two Layer Architecture of Data Warehouse

- The requirement for separation plays a fundamental role in defining the typical architecture for a data warehouse system, as shown in Fig. 1.3.
- Fig. 1.3 shows two-level (two-layer) architecture of data warehouse to highlight the separation of physically available sources and data warehouses. This separation process is important to clean and process operational data, basically it consists of following five stages:
  1. **Data Source:** It is a heterogeneous source data, it might be operational data, flat files, etc.
  2. **Staging Area:** In this area, data stored to sources should be extracted, cleansed to remove inconsistencies and fill gaps before the warehouse.

3. **Warehouse:** It is a centralized repository which can access data directly, but it can also be used as a source for creating data marts.
4. **Data Marts:** Data mart is a partially copy of organization's data and is designed for a specific purpose like purchasing, sales, inventory, etc.
5. **Users:** End users can access the processed report, analyze them and mine them.

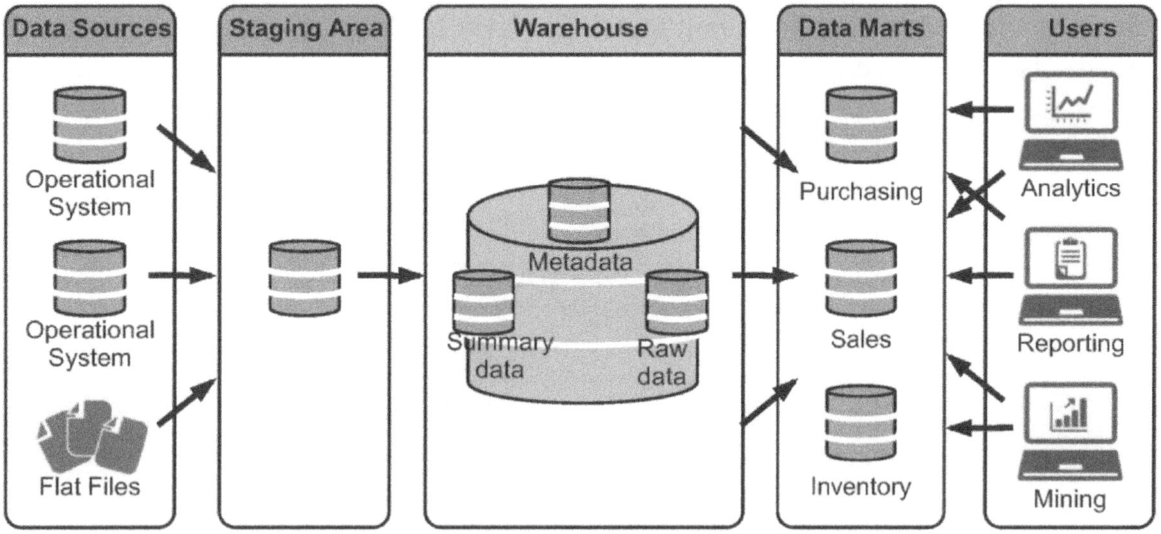

Fig. 1.3 : Two-Level Architecture of Data Warehouse

Benefits of a Two-Layer Architecture:

1. In data warehouse systems, good quality information is always available, even when access to sources is denied temporarily for technical or organizational reasons.
2. Data warehouse analysis queries do not affect the management of transactions, the reliability of which is vital for enterprises to work properly at an operational level.
3. Data warehouses are logically structured according to the multidimensional model, while operational sources are generally based on relational or semi-structured models.

1.3.3 Three Tier Data Warehouse Architecture

- Generally a data warehouses adopts a three tier (layer/level) architecture. Fig. 1.4 shows the three tier architecture of data warehouse.
- Following are the three tiers of the data warehouse architecture:

1. **Bottom Tier:** The bottom tier of the architecture is the data warehouse database server. It is the relational database system. We use the back end tools and utilities to feed data into the bottom tier. These back end tools and utilities perform the Extract, Clean, Load, and refresh functions.

   The following are the functions of data warehouse tools and utilities:

   (i) **Data Extraction:** Involves gathering data from multiple heterogeneous sources.
   (ii) **Data Cleaning:** Involves finding and correcting the errors in data.
   (iii) **Data Transformation:** Involves converting the data from legacy format to warehouse format.
   (iv) **Data Loading:** Involves sorting, summarizing, consolidating, checking integrity, and building indices and partitions.
   (v) **Refreshing:** Involves updating from data sources to warehouse.

2. **Middle Tier:** In the middle tier, we have the OLAP Server that can be implemented in either of the following ways:
   - **(i)** By **Relational OLAP (ROLAP),**which is an extended relational database management system. The ROLAP maps the operations on multidimensional data to standard relational operations.
   - **(ii)** By **Multidimensional OLAP (MOLAP)** model, which directly implements the multidimensional data and operations.
3. **Top Tier:** This tier is the front-end client layer. This layer holds the query tools and reporting tools, analysis tools and data mining tools.

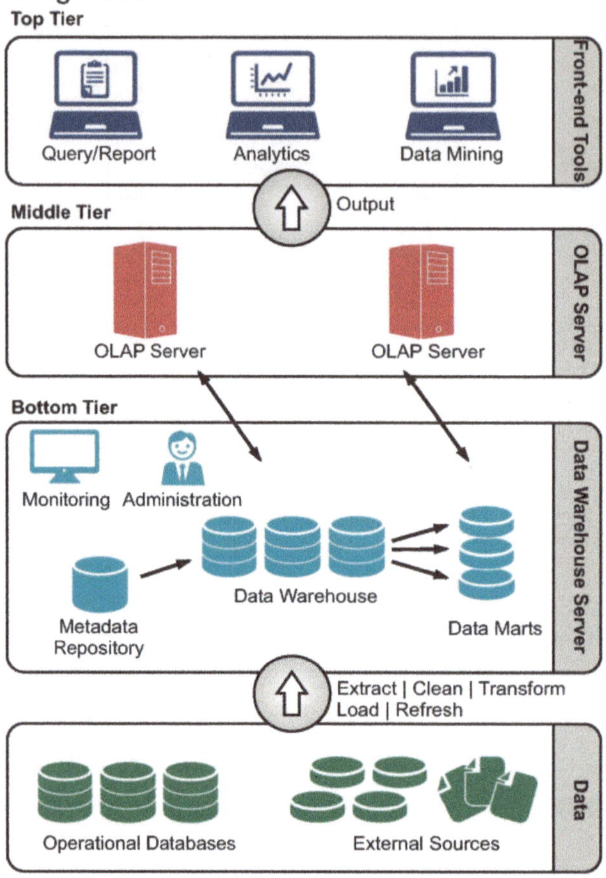

Fig. 1.4: Three Layer Architecture of Data Warehouse

- The main advantage of the reconciled data layer is that it creates a common reference data model for a whole enterprise. At the same time, it sharply separates the problems of source data extraction and integration from those of data warehouse population.

1.4 DATA WAREHOUSE MODEL

- A data warehouse is an electronic system that gathers data from a wide range of sources within a company and uses the data to support management decision-making.
- Data warehouse architecture is changing with time. There are two types of data warehouse architectures, namely, Traditional data Warehouse and Cloud-based architectures.
- Traditional data warehouse architecture employs a three-tier structure, (as explained earlier) composed of the Bottom tier, Middle tier and Top tier.
- In a traditional architecture there are three common data warehouse models are virtual warehouse, data mart, and enterprise data warehouse.
- The cloud-based data warehouses do not adhere to the traditional architecture; each data warehouse offering has a unique architecture.

1.4.1 Virtual Data Warehouse

- The view over an operational data warehouse is known as a virtual warehouse.
- A virtual data warehouse is a set of separate databases, which can be queried together, so a user can effectively access all the data as if it was stored in one data warehouse.
- The operational data warehouse can be a virtual but complex component of an enterprise data warehouse (EDW).
- It is also a multi-purpose structure that enables transactional and decision support processing. Because the data originates from multiple sources, the integration often involves cleaning, resolving redundancy, and checking it against business rules for integrity.

1.4.2 Data Mart

- A data mart is a subset or an aggregation of the data stored to a primary data warehouse. A data mart includes a set of information pieces relevant to a specific business area, corporate department, or category of users.
- A data mart is a subject-specific data warehouse that is usually set up to meet the information needs of users of a particular department or functional unit within an organization. The size of a data in art, therefore, is generally many times smaller than an enterprise data warehouse.
- Data marts contain a subset of organization-wide data that is valuable to specific groups of people in an organization.
- In other words, a data mart contains only those data that is specific to a particular group. For example, the marketing data mart may contain only data related to items, customers and sales. Data marts are confined to subjects.
- A data mart can be called as a subset of a data warehouse or a sub-group of corporate-wide data corresponding to a certain set of users.
- Fig. 1.5 shows a graphical representation of data marts.
- A data mart can be implemented rising a top-down or bottom-up approach. In the former, which is called a **dependent data mart**, data is drawn directly from an enterprise data warehouse. In the latter, which is called an **independent data mart.**
- Individual data marts are built by capturing and transforming data from existing local operational databases in a department or business area.

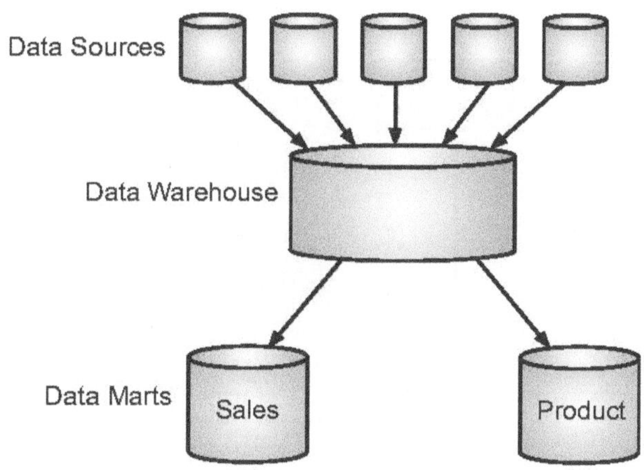

Fig. 1.5: Graphical Representation of Data Marts

Types of Data Mart :

- Depending on the source of data, data marts can be categorized as independent data mart or dependent data mart.
- **Independent data marts** are sourced from data captured from one or more operational systems or external information providers, or from data generated locally within a particular department or geographic area. **Dependent data marts** are sourced directly from enterprise data warehouses.

- A dependent data mart is one whose source is another data warehouse, and all dependent data marts within an organization are typically fed by the same source - the enterprise data warehouse.

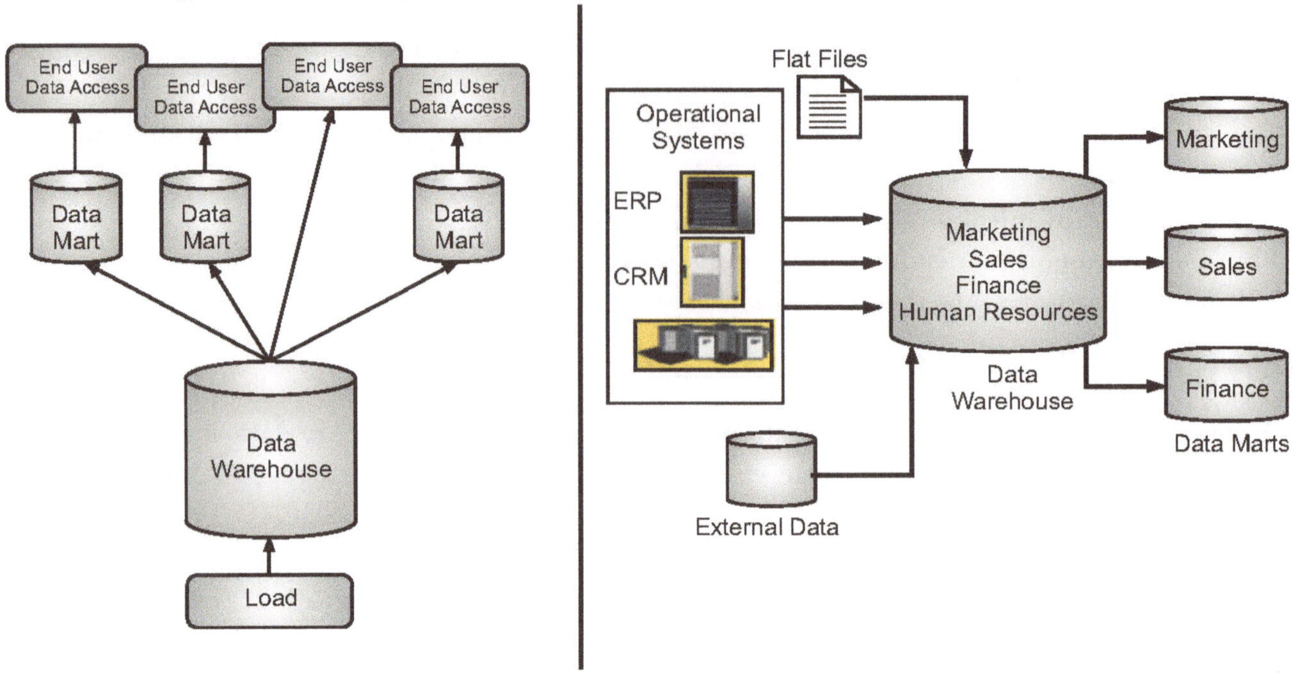

(a) (b)

Fig. 1.6: Dependent Data Mart (Data Mart exists with Data Warehouse)

- An independent data mart is one whose source is directly from transactional systems, legacy applications, or external data feeds. Independent data mart can collect data directly from the different sources.

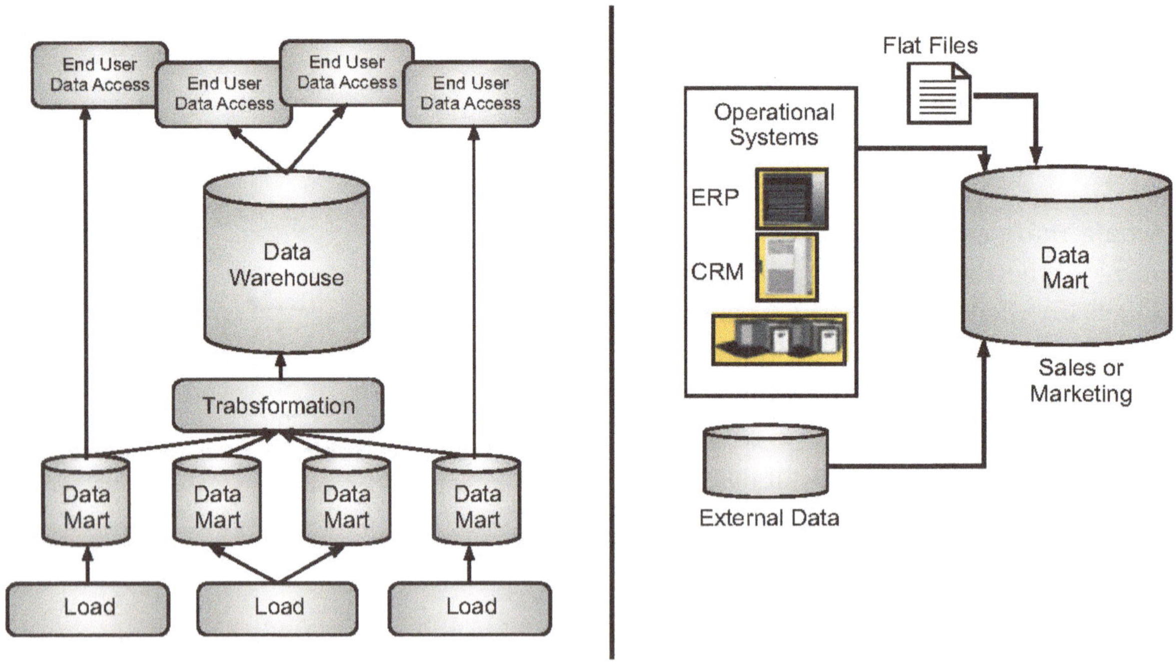

(a) (b)

Fig. 1.7: Independent Data Mart

Advantages of Data Marts:

1. Building a data mart is simpler as compared to implementing a corporate data warehouse.
2. Data marts are small in size.

3. The reporting queries become simpler since filtering is allowed in a data mart. Smaller queries performing on a smaller subset of data are easier to tune in cases of performance enhancement
4. The data marts can be placed on smaller distributed machines to allow users to break away from profoundly powered machines and still handle processing of the reports.
5. The cost of implementing a data mart is far less when compared to build a data warehouse.
6. Data marts are flexible.

Disadvantages of Data Marts:

1. Increase in their size of data marts results in performance deterioration, data inconsistency and creates problems when data warehouse needs to be upgraded.
2. The data marts are frequently short-term, temporary solutions that are not part of a corporate architecture.
3. Development can be unorganized, which creates problems when data marts are used as building blocks for creating an enterprise data warehouse.
4. The process of data access, consolidation and cleaning in data marts becomes very difficult because data marts focus on individual needs.
5. Their design is not as thorough as with a data warehouse due to limited consideration for an ultimate upgrade to an enterprise system.
6. They can be expensive in the long-term process as activities such as extraction and processing can get duplicated. Then, additional persons will be required for maintenance and support.

Difference between Data Warehouse and Data Mart:

Sr. No.	Data Warehouse	Data Mart
1.	Its scope is enterprise-wide.	Its scope is department-wide.
2.	Control and management process of data warehouse is centralized.	Its process is decentralized.
3.	Due to huge amount of data it is complex and difficult to manage and thus, takes long time to produce the result.	Due to fewer amounts of data it is easy to build and manage.
4.	There are many internal and external sources, thus staging design takes much more time.	There are only few internal and external sources and it is self-explanatory; thus it is faster to build.
5.	The data stored inside the data warehouse are always detailed and accurate when compared with data mart.	The data stored inside the data mart is short and limited.
6.	A data warehouse is a large repository of data collected from different organizations.	A data mart is an only subtype of a data warehouse.
7.	Data warehousing includes large area of the corporation which is why it takes a long time to process it.	Data marts are easy to use design and implement as it can only handle small amounts of data.
8.	A data warehouse is a blend of technologies and components which allows the strategic use of data.	A data mart is simple form of a data warehouse. It is focused on a single subject.
9.	It is designed for a long period of time.	It is built with a given objective, and has a short lifespan.

1.4.3 Enterprise Data Warehouse

- An enterprise warehouse collects all of the information about subjects spanning the entire organization. This model sees the data warehouse as the heart of the enterprise's information system, with integrated data from all business units.
- It provides corporate-wide data integration, usually from one or more operational systems or external information providers, and is cross-functional in scope.
- It typically contains detailed data as well as summarized data, and can range in size from a few gigabytes to hundreds of gigabytes, terabytes, or beyond.
- An enterprise data warehouse may be implemented on traditional mainframes, computer super servers, or parallel architecture platforms. It requires extensive business modeling and may take years to design and build.
- The goal of EDW is to provide a complete overview of any particular object in the data model. This is accomplished by identifying and wrangling the data from different systems. This is then loaded into a consistent and conformed model.
- After all the information is gathered by EDW which has the capability of providing access to a single location where different tools can be used to perform analytical functions and create different predictions. The research teams can identify new trends or patterns and focus on them to help the business grow.

1.5 EXTRACTION, TRANSFORMATION AND LOADING (ETL)

- The ETL process encompasses data extraction, transformation, and loading.
- ETL tools are very important because they help in combining Logic, Raw Data and Schema into one and loads the information to the Data Warehouse or Data Marts.

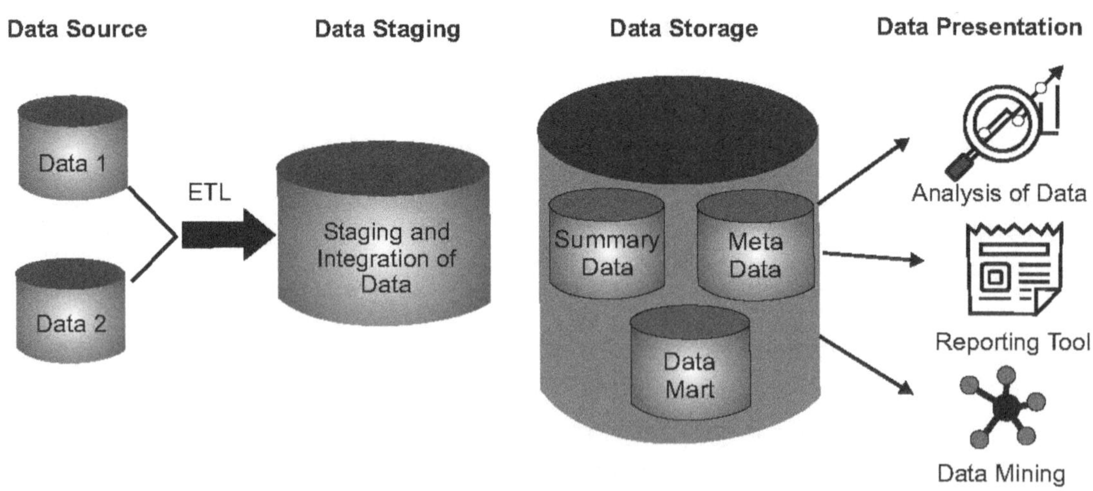

Fig. 1.8: ETL

- Sometimes, ETL loads the data into the Data Marts and then information is stored in Data Warehouse. This approach is known as the Bottom-up approach.
- The approach where ETL loads information to the Data Warehouse directly is known as Top-down Approach.

Difference between Top-down Approach and Bottom-up Approach

Sr. No.	Top-Down Approach	Bottom-Up Approach
1.	Provides a definite and consistent view of information as information from the data warehouse is used to create data marts.	Reports can be generated easily as Data marts are created first and it is relatively easy to interact with data marts.
2.	Strong model and hence preferred by big companies.	Not as strong but data warehouse can be extended and the number of data marts can be created.
3.	Time, cost and maintenance is high.	Time, cost and maintenance are low.

- There are many reasons for adopting ETL in the organization. Some of them are given below :
    1. It helps companies to analyze their business data for taking critical business decisions.
    2. Transactional databases cannot answer complex business questions that can be answered by ETL.
    3. A data warehouse provides a common data repository.
    4. ETL provides a method of moving the data from various sources into a data warehouse.
    5. As data sources change, the Data Warehouse will automatically update.
    6. Well-designed and documented ETL system is almost essential to the success of a Data Warehouse project.
    7. Allow verification of data transformation, aggregation and calculations rules.
    8. ETL process allows sample data comparison between the source and the target system.
    9. ETL process can perform complex transformations and requires the extra area to store the data.
    10. It helps to Migrate data into a Data Warehouse. Convert to the various formats and types to adhere to one consistent system.
    11. It is a predefined process for accessing and manipulating source data into the target database.
    12. ETL offers deep historical context for the business.
    13. It helps to improve productivity because it codifies and reuses without a need for technical skills.

Steps in getting Data into the Data Warehouse:

1. Extraction:

- Extraction is the first step in the process of getting data into the data warehouse environment.
- During extraction, data is specifically identified and then taken from many different locations, referred to as the Source.
- The Source can be a variety of things, such as files, spreadsheets, database tables, a pipe, etc.
- Relevant data is obtained from sources in the extraction phase.
- Extracting means reading and understanding the source data and copying the data needed into the ETL system for further manipulation. At this point, the data belongs to the data warehouse.
- There are two types of data warehouse extraction methods, namely, logical and physical extraction methods as shown in Fig. 1.9.

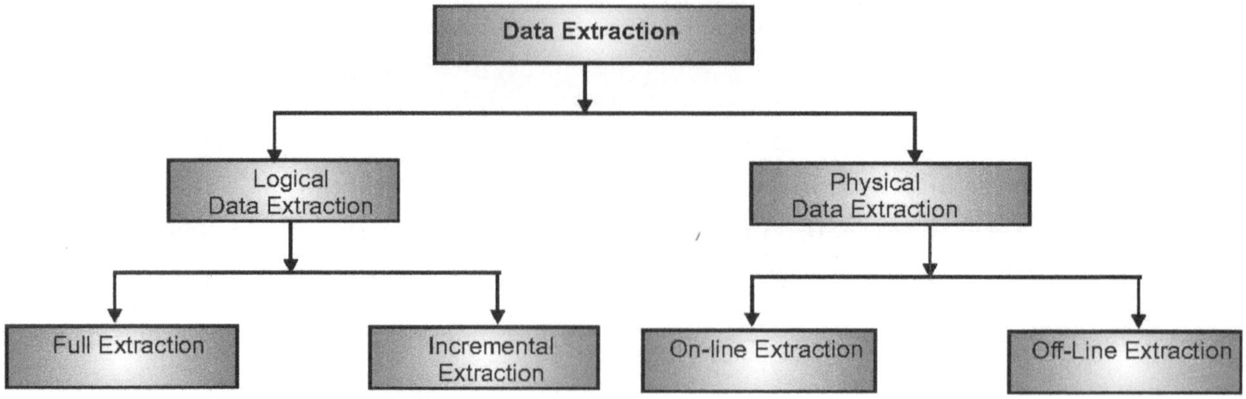

Fig. 1.9

(I) Logical Extraction:

- Logical Extraction method in-turn has two methods:
  - **(i) Full Extraction:** Full extraction is used when the data needs to be extracted and loaded for the first time. In full extraction, the data from the source is extracted completely. This extraction reflects the current data available in the source system.
  - **(ii) Incremental Extraction:** In incremental extraction, the changes in source data need to be tracked since the last successful extraction. Only these changes in data will be extracted and then loaded. These changes can be detected from the source data which have the last changed timestamp. Also a change table can be created in the source system, which keeps track of the changes in the source data.

(II) Physical Extraction:

- Physical extraction has two methods: OnLine and Offline extraction:
  - **(i) OnLine Extraction:** In this process, extraction process directly connect to the source system and extract the source data.
  - **(ii) Offline Extraction:** The data is not extracted directly from the source system but is staged explicitly outside the original source system.

2. Transformation:

- After data is extracted, it must be physically transported to the target destination and converted into the appropriate format.
- It converts data from its operational source format into a specific data warehouse format.
- This data transformation may include operations such as cleaning, joining, and validating data or generating calculated data based on existing values.
- Whether the transformation takes place in the data warehouse or beforehand, there are both common and advanced transformation types that prepare data for analysis.
- Some of these include:

Basic transformations:

- **(i) Cleaning:** Mapping NULL to 0 or "Male" to "M" and "Female" to "F," date format consistency, etc.
- **(ii) Deduplication:** Identifying and removing duplicate records.
- **(iii) Format Revision:** Character set conversion, unit of measurement conversion, date/time conversion, etc.
- **(iv) Key Restructuring:** Establishing key relationships across tables.

Advanced transformations:

(i) **Derivation:** Applying business rules to the data that derive new calculated values from existing data – for example, creating a revenue metric that subtracts taxes.

(ii) **Filtering:** Selecting only certain rows and/or columns.

(iii) **Joining:** Linking data from multiple sources – for example, adding ad spend data across multiple platforms, such as Google Adwords and Facebook Ads.

(iv) **Splitting:** Splitting a single column into multiple columns.

(v) **Data Validation:** Simple or complex data validation – for example, if the first three columns in a row are empty then reject the row from processing.

(vi) **Summarization:** Values are summarized to obtain total figures which are calculated and stored at multiple levels as business metrics – for example, adding up all purchases a customer has made to build a Customer Lifetime Value (CLV) metric.

(vii) **Aggregation:** Data elements are aggregated from multiple data sources and databases.

(viii)**Integration:** Give each unique data element one standard name with one standard definition. Data integration reconciles different data names and values for the same data element.

3. Loading:

- Loading into a data warehouse is the last step to take. The final step in the ETL process involves loading the transformed data into the destination target.
- This target may be a database or a data warehouse. Loading can be carried out in two ways namely full load and incremental load.
  (i) The **full load** method involves an entire data dump that occurs the first time the source is loaded into the warehouse.
  (ii) The **incremental load**, on the other hand, takes place at regular intervals. These intervals can be streaming increments (better for smaller data volumes) or batch increments (better for larger data volumes).
- There two different methods of loading data into a warehouse are given in following table:

ETL	ELT
• Extract, Transform, Load (ETL) first extracts the data from a pool of data sources, which are typically transactional databases. • The data is held in a temporary staging database. Transformation operations are then performed, to structure and convert the data into a suitable form for the target data warehouse system. • The structured data is then loaded into the warehouse, ready for analysis.	• With Extract Load Transform (ELT), data is immediately loaded after being extracted from the source data pools. • There is no staging database, meaning the data is immediately loaded into the single, centralized repository. • The data is transformed inside the data warehouse system for use with business intelligence tools and analytics.

ETL	ELT
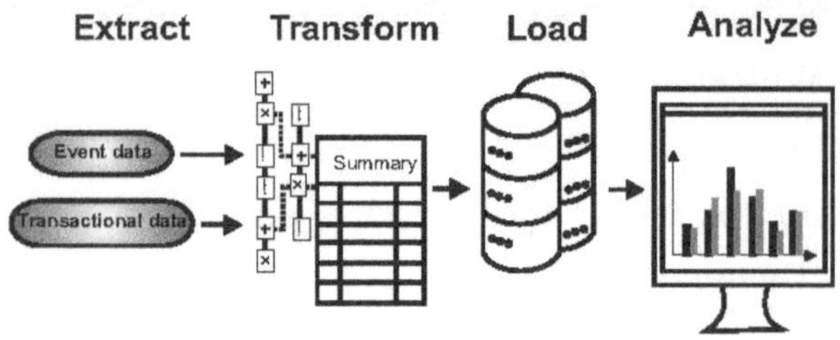	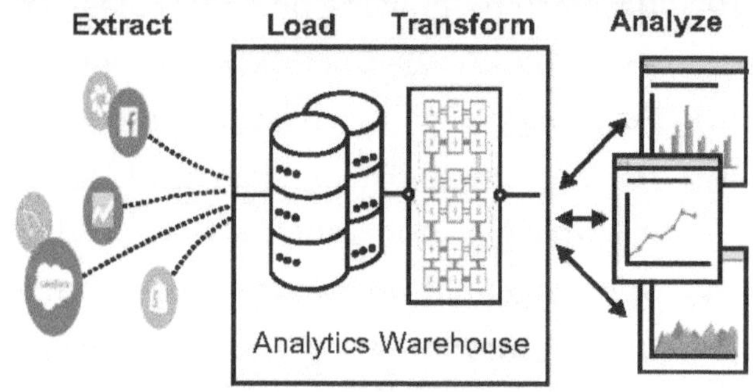
• Traditional approach for analysis of data is ETL.	• Modern approach for analysis of Data is ELT.

1.6 METADATA REPOSITORY

- Metadata is simply defined as, data about data. The data that are used to represent other data is know as metadata. For example, the index of a book serves as metadata for the contents in the book.
- In other words we can say that metadata is the summarized data that leads us to the detailed data.
- In terms of data warehouse we can define metadata as:
    1. Metadata is a road map to data warehouse.
    2. Metadata in data warehouse define the warehouse objects.
    3. The metadata act as a directory. This directory helps the decision support system to locate the contents of data warehouse.
- Metadata in a data warehouse is similar to the data dictionary or the data catalog in a database management system.
- In the data dictionary, we keep the information about the logical data structures, the information about the files and addresses, the information about the indexes, and so on. The data dictionary contains data about the data in the database.
- The metadata can be broadly categorized into following three categories:
    1. **Business Metadata:** This metadata has the data ownership information, business definition and changing policies.
    2. **Technical Metadata:** Technical metadata includes database system names, table and column names and sizes, data types and allowed values. Technical metadata also includes structural information such as primary and foreign key attributes and indices.
    3. **Operational Metadata:** This metadata includes currency of data and data lineage. Currency of data means whether data is active, archived or purged. Lineage of data means history of data migrated and transformation applied on it.
- In the data warehouse architecture, meta-data plays an important role as it specifies the source, usage, values, and features of data warehouse data. It also defines how data can be changed and processed. It is closely connected to the data warehouse.
- The generation and management of metadata serves two purposes:

1. **To Minimize the Efforts for Development and Administration of a Data Warehouse as Metadata** provide following information:
   (i) Information on the contents of the data warehouse, their location and their structure,
   (ii) Information on the processes that take place in the data warehouse back-stage, concerning the refreshment of the warehouse with clean, up-to-date, semantically and structurally reconciled data,
   (iii) Information on the implicit semantics of data (with respect to a common enterprise model), along with any other kind of data that aids the end-user exploit the information of the warehouse,
   (iv) Information on the infrastructure and physical characteristics of components and the sources of the data warehouse, and,
   (v) Information including security, authentication, and usage statistics that aids the administrator tune the operation of the data warehouse as appropriate.
2. **To improve the Extraction of Information as Metadata:**
   (i) Improves data quality like consistency (uniform and no duplicates), completeness (whether data is missing), accuracy (precision and confidence of the data), timeliness (value is up-to-date).
   (ii) Improves query, retrieval and answer quality.
   (iii) Improves data analysis.

- Metadata has very important role in data warehouse. The role of metadata in warehouse is different from the warehouse data yet it has very important role. The various roles of metadata are explained below:
  1. The metadata act as a directory.
  2. Metadata are also used for query tools.
  3. Metadata are used in reporting tools.
  4. Metadata are used in extraction and cleansing tools.
  5. Metadata are used in transformation tools.
  6. Metadata also plays important role in loading functions.
  7. The directory helps the decision support system to locate the contents of data warehouse.
  8. Metadata helps in decision support system for mapping of data when data are transformed from operational environment to data warehouse environment.
  9. Metadata helps in summarization between current detailed data and highly summarized data.
  10. Metadata also helps in summarization between lightly detailed data and highly summarized data.
- A metadata repository is a database of data about data (metadata). A metadata repository is used in the bottom tier of the data warehousing architecture.
- The purpose of the metadata repository is to provide a consistent and reliable means of access to data. The repository itself may be stored in a physical location or may be a virtual database, in which metadata is drawn from separate sources.
- Metadata repository is just like a general-purpose information directory or catalogying device which is used for classifying, storing and managing metadata.
- A metadata repository should contain the following:

1. A description of the **data warehouse structure**, which includes the warehouse schema, view, dimensions, hierarchies, and derived data definitions, as well as data mart locations and contents.
2. **Operational metadata,** which include data lineage (history of migrated data and the sequence of transformations applied to it), currency of data (active, archived, or purged), and monitoring information (warehouse usage statistics, error reports, and audit trails).
3. The **algorithms used for summarization**, which include measure and dimension definition algorithms, data on granularity, partitions, subject areas, aggregation, summarization, and predefined queries and reports.
4. **Mapping from the operational environment to the data warehouse**, which includes source databases and their contents, gateway descriptions, data partitions, data extraction, cleaning, transformation rules and defaults, data refresh and purging rules, and security (user authorization and access control).
5. **Data related to system performance**, which include indices and profiles that improve data access and retrieval performance, in addition to rules for the timing and scheduling of refresh, update, and replication cycles.
6. **Business metadata,** which include business terms and definitions, data ownership information, and charging policies.

1.7 BENEFITS OF DATA WAREHOUSING

- Various benefits of data warehousing are given below:
  1. **Improved Control of Data:** Information in the data warehouse is under the control of data warehouse users so that, even if the source system data is removed over time, the information in the warehouse can be stored safely for extended periods of time.
  2. **Better Retrieval of Data:** Because they are separate from operational systems, data warehouses provide retrieval of data without slowing down operational systems.
  3. **Increased Productivity of Corporate Decision Makers:** Data warehousing improves the productivity of corporate decision makers by creating an integrated database of consistent, subject-oriented, historical data. It integrates data from multiple incompatible systems into a form that provides one consistent view of the organization. By transforming data into meaningful information, a data warehouse allows business managers to perform more substantive, accurate, and consistent analysis.
  4. **More Cost-Effective Decision-Making:** Data warehousing helps to reduce the overall cost of the product by reducing the number of channels.
  5. **Better Enterprise Intelligence:** It helps to provide better enterprise intelligence and enhanced customer service.
  6. **Potential High Returns on Investment:** Return on investment (ROI) refers to the amount of increased revenue. Implementations of data warehouses and complementary business intelligence systems have enabled business to generate higher amounts of revenue and provide substantial cost savings.

7. **Competitive Advantage:** The huge returns on investment for those companies/organizations that have successfully implemented a data warehouse is evidence of the enormous competitive advantage that accompanies this technology. The competitive advantage is gained by allowing decision-makers access to data that can reveal previously unavailable, unknown, and untapped information on, for example, customers, trends, and demands.

Limitations of Data Warehouse:

1. **Hidden Problems with Source Systems:** Sometimes hidden problems associated with the source systems feeding the data warehouse may be identified after years of being undetected. For example, when entering the details of a new property, certain fields may allow nulls which may result in staff entering incomplete property data, even when available and applicable.
2. **Required Data Not Captured:** In some cases the required data is not captured by the source systems which may be very important for the data warehouse purpose. For example, the date of registration for the property may be not used in source system but it may be very important analysis purpose.
3. **Increased End-User Demands :** Once a data warehouse is OnLine, it is often the case that the number of users and queries increase together with requests for answers to more and more complex queries.
4. **Data Homogenization:** The concept of data warehouse deals with similarity of data formats between different data sources. Thus, results in to lose of some important value of the data.
5. **High Demand for Resources:** The data warehouse requires large amounts of data.
6. **Data Ownership:** Data warehousing may change the attitude of end-users to the ownership of data. Sensitive data that owned by one department has to be loaded in data warehouse for decision making purpose. But some time it results in to reluctance of that department because it may hesitate to share it with others.
7. **High Maintenance:** Data warehouses are high maintenance systems. Any reorganization of the business processes and the source systems may affect the data warehouse and it results high maintenance cost.
8. **Long-Duration Projects:** The building of a warehouse can take up to three years, which is why some organizations are reluctant in investigating in to data warehouse. Whereas, data marts support only the requirements of a particular department and limited the functionality to that department or area only.
9. **Complexity of Integration:** An organization must spend a significant amount of time determining how well the various different data warehousing tools can be integrated into the overall solution that is needed. This can be a very difficult task, as there are a number of tools for every operation of the data warehouse.
10. **Under-Estimation of Resources of Data Loading:** Sometimes, we underestimate the time required to extract, clean, and load the data into the warehouse. It may take the significant proportion of the total development time, although some tools are there which are used to reduce the time and effort spent on this process.

Practice Questions

1. What is data warehouse?
2. What is data warehousing?
3. What is ETC?
4. What is operational database?
5. What is the need of data warehouse?
6. Explain characteristics of Data warehouse.
7. Give 8 differences between operational database and data warehouse
8. Explain components of data warehouse with neat diagram
9. Explain multitier architecture of data warehouse.
10. Explain data warehouse models.
11. What is data mart? Give its types.
12. Give difference between data warehouse and data mart
13. How ETL is helpful in data warehouse?
14. What is metadata repository?
15. List benefits of data warehouse.

✤ ✤ ✤

2...

Data Warehouse Modeling and Online Analytical Processing I

Chapter Outcomes...

- Describe data cube and OLAP for the given data warehouse.
- Explain schemas for multidimensional data models for the given data warehouse.
- Compare stars, snowflakes and schema models for the given data warehouse on the basis of the given criteria.
- Describe the given OLAP operations.
- Explain the benefits of the given OLAP tool.

Learning Objectives...

- To understand Basic Concepts in Data Warehouse Modeling
- To learn Data Cube Model
- To learn Concepts in OLTP (Need, Guidelines etc.)
- To study Typical Operations in OLAP

2.0 INTRODUCTION

- A data model is a graphical view of data created for analysis and design purposes. Data modeling is the process of creating a data model for the data to be stored in a database.
- Data modeling includes designing data warehouse databases in detail, it follows principles and patterns established in architecture for data warehousing.

2.1 DATA WAREHOUSE MODELING

- Data warehouse modeling is the process of designing the schemas of the detailed and summarized information of the data warehouse.
- The goal of data warehouse modeling is to develop a schema describing the reality, or at least a part of the fact, which the data warehouse is needed to support.
- Data model emphasizes on what data is needed and how it should be organized instead of what operations need to be performed on the data.
- Data warehouse uses a data model that is based on a multidimensional data model. This model is also known as a data cube.

- The data cube model allows data to be modeled and viewed in multiple dimensions. Dimensions are the different perspectives for an entity that an organization is interested in.
- OnLine Analytical Processing (OLAP) is based on the multidimensional data model. OLAP enables users to access information from multidimensional data warehouses almost instantly, to view information in any way they like, and to cleanly specify and carry out sophisticated calculations.
- OLAP data is typically stored in a star schema or snowflake schema or fact constellation schema in a relational data warehouse. Schema is a logical description of the entire database.
- Each dimension in a star schema is represented with only one-dimension table. This dimension table contains the set of attributes. The dimensions table in a snowflake schema are normalized. A fact constellation has multiple fact tables. It is also known as galaxy schema.
- Dimensional modeling represents data with a cube operation, making more suitable logical data representation with OLAP data management.
- A data cube helps us represent data in multiple dimensions. It is defined by dimensions and facts. The dimensions are the entities with respect to which an enterprise preserves the records.

2.1.1 Data Cube and OLAP

- Data warehouses and OLAP tools are based on a multidimensional data model. This model views data in the form of a data cube.
- A data cube allows data to be modeled and viewed in multiple dimensions. It is defined by dimensions and facts/measures.

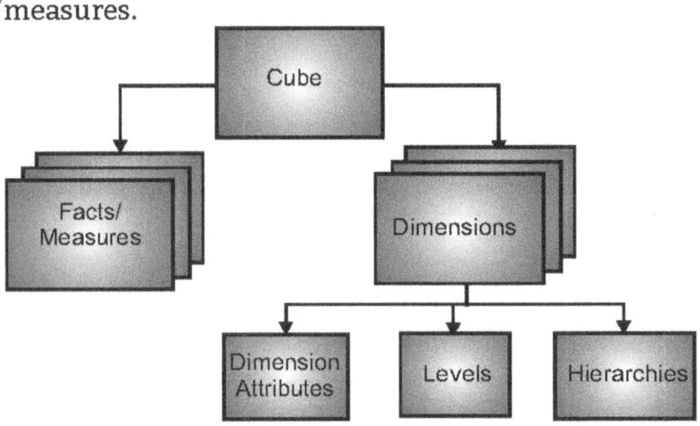

Fig. 2.1

- A data cube is a data structure that allows fast data analysis. Data cube contain two basic types of data as shown in Fig. 2.2.

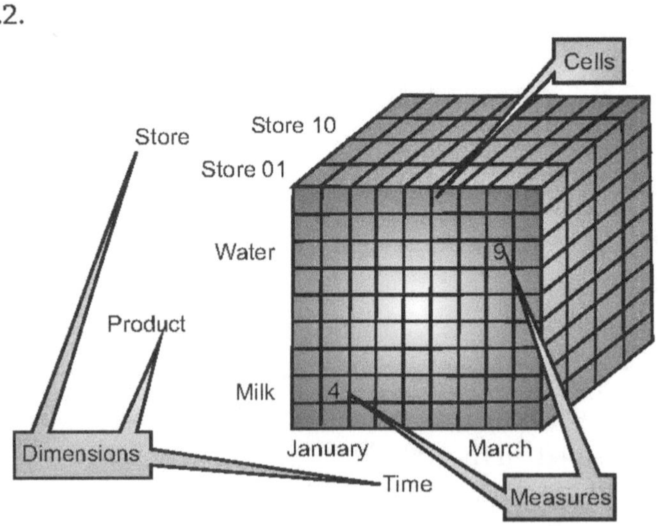

Fig. 2.2

1. **Facts or Measures**, which are integer or decimal values that can be accessed either at the detailed dimension member level or can be aggregated at higher dimension levels in data cube. Facts or Measures are the central values in the OLAP that are preprocessed, aggregated, and analyzed. Typical fact/measure examples could be Sales amount, Units sold, Cost amount, Transactions count etc.
2. **Dimensions**, which are the categories that we use to organize the facts or measures. Dimensions consist of and dimension attributes, levels and hierarchies.

Dimension Attributes:

- An attribute provides additional information about the data. Some attributes are used for display. We might also have attributes like colors, flavors, or sizes.

Hierarchy:

- A logical tree structure that organizes the members of a dimension such that each member has one parent member and zero or more child members.
- For example, a time dimension might include a hierarchy with levels for Year, Quarter, Month, and Day.
  - A child is a member in the next lower level in a hierarchy that is directly related to the current member. For example, in a Time hierarchy containing the levels Quarter, Month, and Day, January is a child of Qtr1.
  - A parent is a member in the next higher level in a hierarchy that is directly related to the current member. The parent value is usually a consolidation of the values of all of its children. For example, in a Time hierarchy that contains the levels Quarter, Month, and Day, Qtr1 is the parent of January.

Level:

- Within a hierarchy, data can be organized into lower and higher levels of detail, such as Year, Quarter, Month, and Day levels in a Time hierarchy.
- Another example is, a geography dimension might include levels for Country, State, and City.

2.1.2 Data Cube

- Data cubes are multidimensional extensions of 2D tables, like as in geometry a cube is a three-dimensional extension of a square.
- Data cubes are not restricted to just three dimensions. Most OnLine Analytical Processing (OLAP) systems can build data cubes with many more dimensions.
- Data cube is data structure that aggregates the measures by the levels and hierarchies of each of the dimensions that we want to analyze.
- Cubes combine several dimensions, such as time, geography, and product lines, with summarized data, such as sales or inventory figures.
- The data cube summarizes the measure with respect to a set of n dimensions and provides summarizations for all subsets of them as shown in Fig. 2.3.
- The most detailed part of the cube is called a base cuboid. The top most 0-D cuboid, which holds the highest-level of summarization, is called the apex cuboid. The lattice of cuboids forms a data cube.
- A data cube, such as sales, allows data to be modeled and viewed in multiple dimensions. Each dimension may have a table associated with it, called a dimension table, which further describes the dimension.

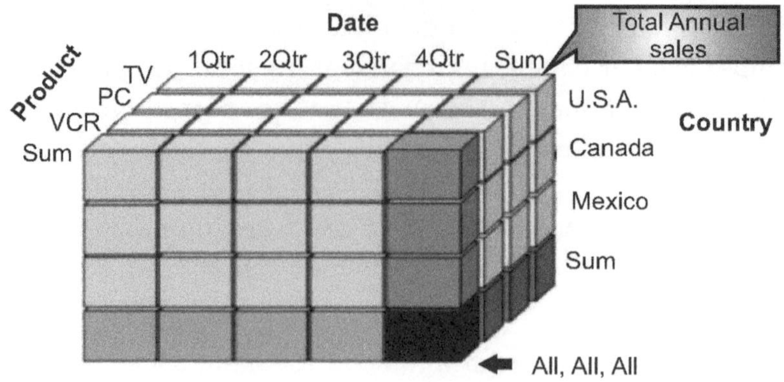

(a) A sample Data Cube

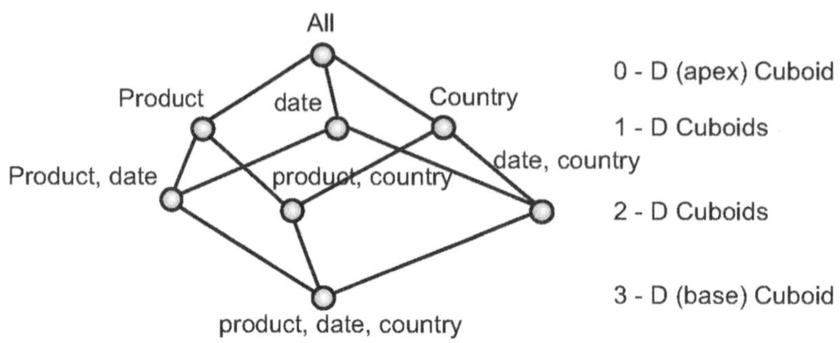

(b) Cuboids of the Sample Cube

Fig. 2.3

- For example,
  - A dimension table name is item consist of item name, brand and type.
  - A dimension table name is time consist of day, week, month, quarter and year.
- Dimension tables can be specified by users or experts, or automatically generated and adjusted based on data distributions.
- A multidimensional data model is typically organized around a central theme, such as *sales*. This theme is represented by a fact table. Fact table contains facts/measures (such as dollars_sold) and keys to each of the related dimension tables.

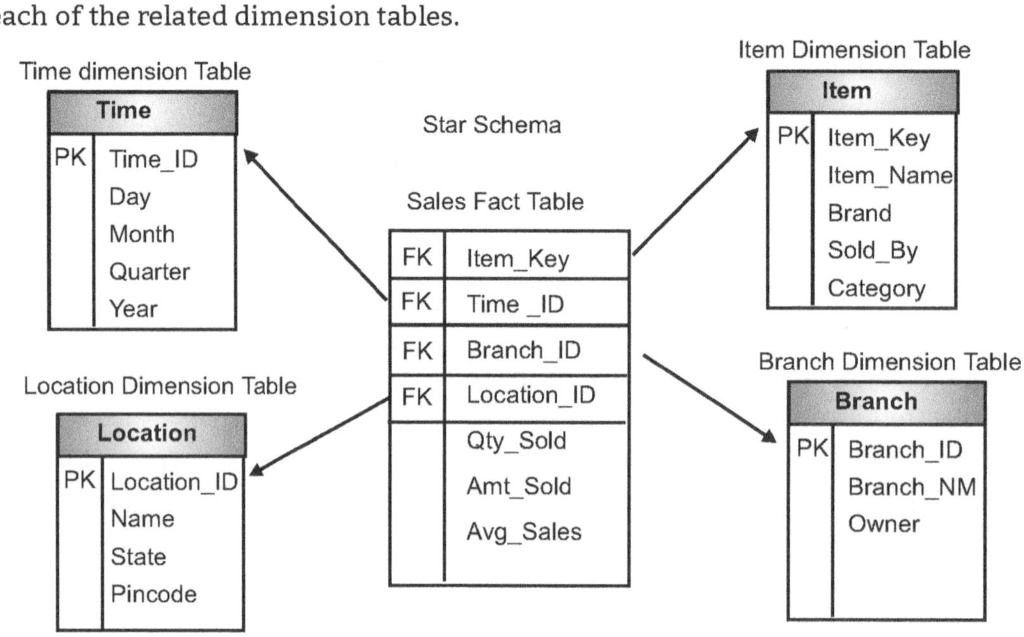

Fig. 2.4

- It contains all the primary keys of the dimension and associated facts or measures (is a property on which calculations can be made) like quantity sold, amount sold and average sales.
- Here, Dimension tables provides descriptive information for all the measurements recorded in fact table. Dimensions are relatively very small as comparison of fact table.

Difference between Fact Table and Dimension Table:

Sr. No.	Characteristics	Fact Table	Dimension Table
1.	Basic Definition	It contains measurements facts or metrics of the attributes.	It is the companion table that contains attributes using which fact table deduce the facts.
2.	Design	It is defined by data grain.	It is descriptive, complete the wordy.
3.	Task	It contains measures and is used for analysis and decision making.	It contains information about a business and its process.
4.	Type of Data	It contains data in both numeric as well as textual format.	It contains data in only textual format.
5.	Key	It has a Primary Key (PK) for each dimension which is acts as a Foreign Key (FK) in the dimension table.	It has a Foreign Key (FK) associated with the Primary Key (PK) of the fact table.
6.	Storage	It stores the filter domain and reports labels in dimension tables.	It stores detailed atomic data into dimensional structures.
7.	Hierarchy	It does not have a hierarchy.	It contains a hierarchy.
8.	Attributes	It has less attributes.	More attributes.
9.	Records	More records.	Less records.
10.	Table Growth	The table grows vertically.	The table grows horizontally.
11.	Creation Time	A fact table is created after dimension tables are created.	The dimension table needs to be created first.
12.	Schema Structure	There is less number of fact tables in a schema.	There is a number of dimension tables in a schema.

2.2 A MULTIDIMENSIONAL DATA MODEL

- Data cubes facilitate the Online analytical processing of multidimensional data. Mostly, data warehousing supports two or three-dimensional cubes.
- A data cube allows data to be viewed in multiple dimensions. Dimensions are entities with respect to which an organization wants to keep records.
- For example, in store sales record, dimensions allow the store to keep track of things like monthly sales of items and the branches and locations.

- A multidimensional database helps to provide data-related answers to complex business queries quickly and accurately.
- Data warehouses and OnLine Analytical Processing (OLAP) tools are based on a multidimensional data model. OLAP in data warehousing enables users to view data from different angles and dimensions.
- Relational data models are used by data bases for their logical structure while multidimensional data model uses schema for the same purpose.
- Schema in general terms means "logical structure". So, data warehouse schema describes the logical structure of any data warehouse containing records.

2.2.1 Star Schemas for Multidimensional Model

- The simplest data warehouse schema is star schema because its structure resembles a star. Star schema consists of data in the form of facts and dimensions.
- In the Star schema, the center of the star can have one fact tables and numbers of associated dimension tables.
- The fact table present in the center of star and points of the star are the dimension tables.
- In star schema fact table contain a large amount of data, with no redundancy. Each dimension table is joined with the fact table using a primary or foreign key.
- It is also known as Star Join Schema and is optimized for querying large data sets.
- The main characteristics of star schema are that it is easy to understand and small number of tables can join.

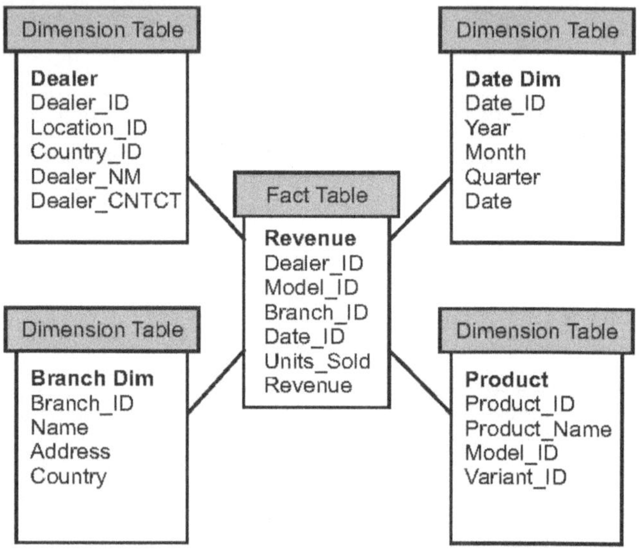

Fig. 2.5: Star Schemas for Multidimensional Model

Advantages:

1. Highly optimized performance.
2. Applicable on both large scale data sources(such as databases) as well as small scale data sources (such as data marts).
3. Star schema is simple and easy to maintain.

Disadvantages:

1. Lesser accuracy and consistency.
2. De-normalized data.
3. Data Redundancy.

2.2.2 Snowflake Schemas for Multidimensional Model

- The snowflake schema is a more complex than star schema because dimension tables of the snowflake are normalized.
- The snowflake schema is represented by centralized fact table which is connected to multiple dimension table and this dimension table can be normalized into additional dimension tables.
- The major difference between the snowflake and star schema models is that the dimension tables of the snowflake model are normalized to reduce redundancies.

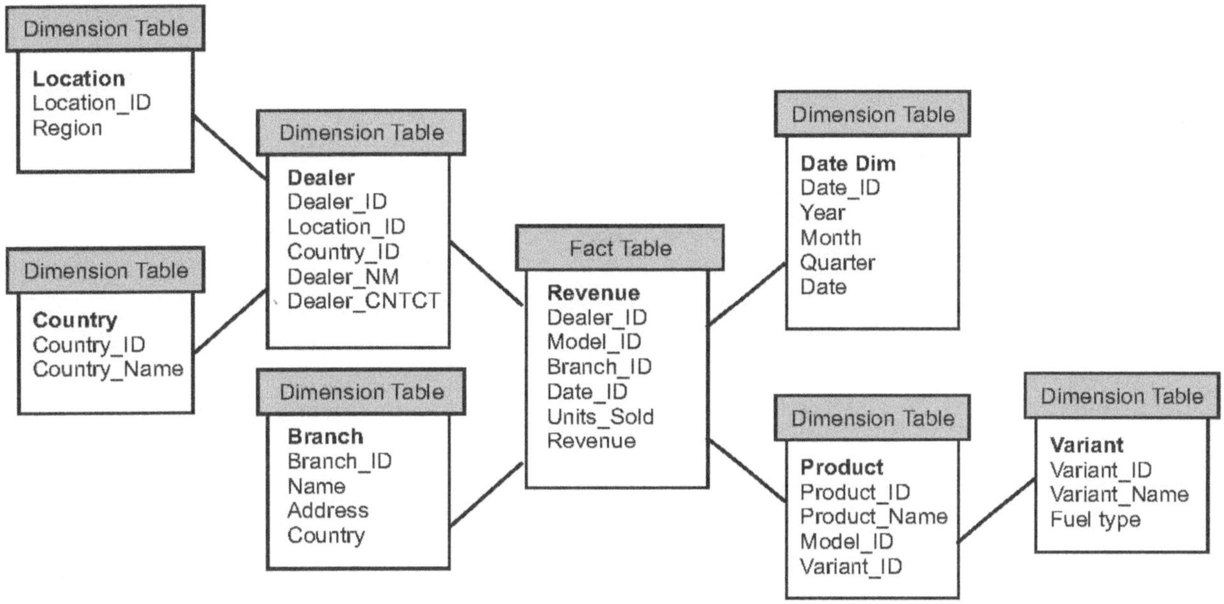

Fig. 2.6 : Snowflake Schemas for Multidimensional Model

Advantages:

1. Lesser data redundancy.
2. Normalized data usage.
3. More accurate and consistent than star schema.

Disadvantages:

1. Slower as compared to star schema due to use of joins.
2. More complex than star schema.
3. More complex queries are required because of use of joins.

2.2.3 Fact Constellation Schemas for Multidimensional Modal

- A fact constellation can have multiple fact tables that share many dimension tables.
- This type of schema can be viewed as a collection of stars, Snowflake and hence is called a galaxy schema or a fact constellation.
- The main disadvantage of fact constellation schemas is its more complicated design.

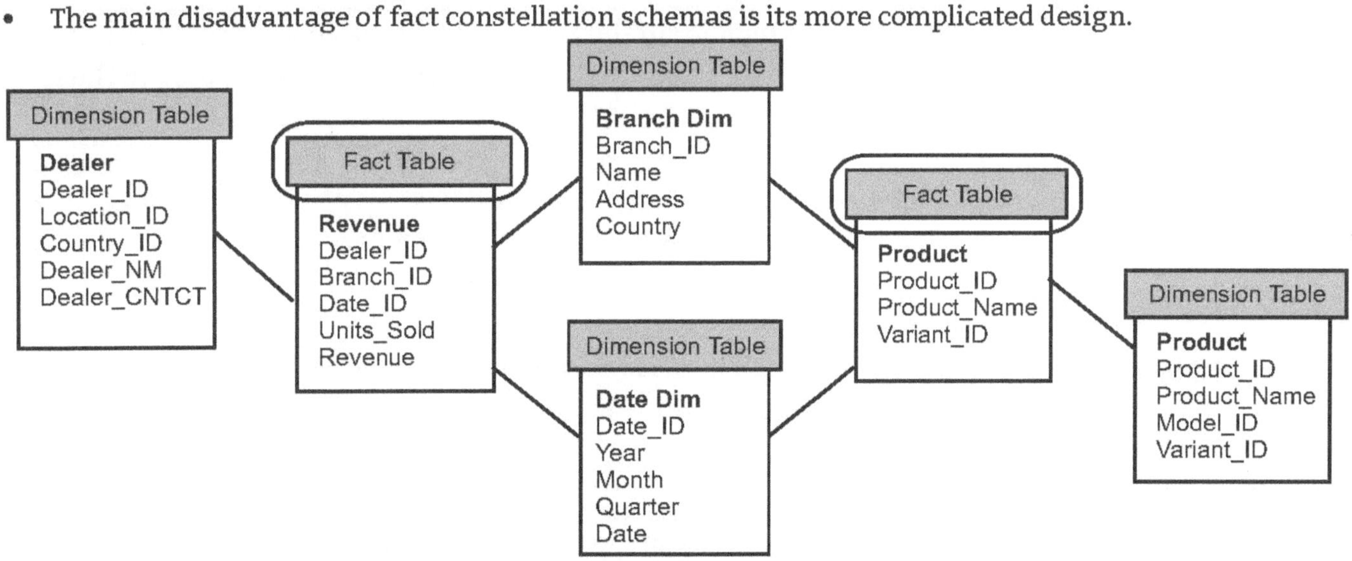

Fig. 2.7 : Fact Constellation Schemas for Multidimensional Model

Advantages:

1. Highly flexible.
2. No data redundancy.
3. Low memory/space required.

Disadvantages:

1. Complicated design.
2. To create, implement and maintain galaxy schema is a tough job.
3. More complex queries are required because of higher number of joins used to connect fact and dimension tables.
4. Data analysis is difficult because of complex structure.

2.3 OLAP

- OLAP stands for OnLine Analytical Processing. The first attempt to provide a definition to OLAP was by Dr. E. F. Codd, who proposed 12 rules (explained later in this chapter) for OLAP.

Types of OLAP:

- There are mainly two types of OLAP namely, Multidimensional OLAP (MOLAP) and Relational OLAP (ROLAP). The combination of MOLAP and ROLAP is called Hybrid OLAP (HOLAP).

1. ROLAP:

- ROLAP stands for Relational OnLine Analytical Processing system. As the name suggests, ROLAP deals with the data present in any relational database.
- Relational database means, database whose data is represented or stored in the form of tables (Fields with rows and columns).
- For large scalable data, ROLAP servers can be used because of its high query processing ability which is capable of generating required/desired results. SQL is the most common query language that is used in ROLAP servers for result extraction.

2. MOLAP:

- MOLAP stands for Multidimensional OnLine Analytical Processing system. The major difference between ROLAP and MOLAP is, ROLAP is used when data is large whereas MOLAP is used when data scale is small.
- In MOLAP, data is stored in summarized manner in the form of data cube where every dimension of the data cube represents an attribute of data stored in it, as compared to the data stored in the form of tables in ROLAP.
- MOLAP system works on the concept of data cube. As data cube offer a number of views of data available in the data cube which can result in better decision making. Also, this can lead to data redundancy as every dimension might occur common in the different views.

2.3.1 Need of OLAP

- OnLine Analytical Processing Server (OLAP) is based on the multidimensional data model. It allows managers, and analysts to get an insight of the information through fast, consistent, and interactive access to information.

Characteristics of OLAP Systems:

1. Provide the business users to have a multidimensional and logical view of the data in the data warehouse.

2. Facilitate interactive query and complex analysis for the users.
3. Allow users to drill down for greater details or roll up for aggregations of metrics along a single business dimension or across multiple dimensions.
4. Provide ability to perform complex calculations and comparisons.
5. Present results in a number of meaningful ways, including charts and graphs.

- Following are the some of the benefits of OLAP systems:
  1. Increased productivity of business managers, executives and analysts.
  2. Inherent flexibility of OLAP systems means that users may be self-sufficient in running their own analysis without IT assistance.
  3. Benefit for IT developers because using software specifically designed for the system development results in faster delivery of applications.
  4. Self-sufficiency of users, resulting in reduction in backlog.
  5. Faster delivery of applications following from the previous benefits.
  6. More efficient operations through reducing time on query executions and in network traffic.
  7. Ability to model real-world challenges with business metrics and dimensions.

2.3.2 OLAP Guidelines

- In 1993, Dr. Edgar F. Codd originated twelve rules as the basis for selecting OLAP tools. OLAP guidelines created by his own which according to him a database must obey to be regarded as a true relational database.
- Following are the Dr. E. F. Codd' twelve (12) **guidelines** for an OLAP system:
  1. **Multidimensional Conceptual View:** Provide a multidimensional data model that is intuitively analytical and easy to use. Business users' view of an enterprise is multidimensional in nature. Therefore, a multidimensional data model conforms to how the users perceive business problems.
  2. **Transparency:** Make the technology, underlying data repository, computing architecture and the diverse nature of source data totally transparent to users. Such transparency, supporting a true open system approach, helps to enhance the efficiency and productivity of the users through front-end tools that are familiar to them.
  3. **Accessibility:** Provide access only to the data that is actually needed to perform the specific analysis, presenting a single, coherent, and consistent view to the users. The OLAP system must map its own logical schema to the heterogeneous physical data stores and perform any necessary transformations.
  4. **Consistent Reporting Performance:** Ensure that the users do not experience any significant degradation in reporting performance as the number of dimensions or the size of the database increases. Users must perceive consistent run time, response time, or machine utilization every time a given query is run.
  5. **Client/Server Architecture:** Conform the system to the principles of client/server architecture for optimum performance, flexibility, adaptability, and interoperability. Make the server component sufficiently intelligent to enable various clients to be attached with a minimum of effort and integration programming.
  6. **Generic Dimensionality:** Ensure that every data dimension is equivalent in both structure and operational capabilities. Have one logical structure for all dimensions. The basic data structure or the access techniques must not be biased toward any single data dimension.
  7. **Dynamic Sparse Matrix Handling:** Adapt the physical schema to the specific analytical model being created and loaded that optimizes sparse matrix handling. When encountering a sparse

matrix, the system must be able to dynamically deduce the distribution of the data and adjust the storage and access to achieve and maintain consistent level of performance.

8. **Multiuser Support:** Provide support for end users to work concurrently with either the same analytical model or to create different models from the same data. In short, provide concurrent data access, data integrity, and access security.
9. **Unrestricted Cross-dimensional Operations:** Provide ability for the system to recognize dimensional hierarchies and automatically perform roll-up and drill-down operations within a dimension or across dimensions. Have the interface language allow calculations and data manipulations across any number of data dimensions, without restricting any relations between data cells, regardless of the number of common data attributes each cell contains.
10. **Intuitive Data Manipulation:** Enable consolidation path reorientation (pivoting), drill-down and roll-up, and other manipulations to be accomplished intuitively and directly via point-and-click and drag-and-drop actions on the cells of the analytical model. Avoid the use of a menu or multiple trips to a user interface.
11. **Flexible Reporting:** Provide capabilities to the business user to arrange columns, rows, and cells in a manner that facilitates easy manipulation, analysis, and synthesis of information. Every dimension, including any subsets, must be able to be displayed with equal ease.
12. **Unlimited Dimensions and Aggregation Levels:** Accommodate at least fifteen, preferably twenty, data dimensions within a common analytical model. Each of these generic dimensions must allow a practically unlimited number of user-defined aggregation levels within any given consolidation path.

- Many data warehouse projects are under funded, unfocused, end-users are not trained to access data effectively, or there are organizational issues that cause them to fail. In fact, a large number of data warehousing projects which fail during the first year.
- According to Mitch Kramer, consulting editor at Patricia Seybold Group, strategic technologies, best practices, and business solutions consulting group based in Boston, there are many ways to make a data warehouse successful.
- Here are a few of the areas to be aware of when creating and implementing a data warehouse:

1. **Keep Things Focused:** "Try not to create a global solution." Kramer suggests that a good practice is to "focus on what you need. A small data warehouse or data mart which addresses a single subject or that is focused on a single department is much more efficient than a large data warehouse. You will see measurable results much faster from a data mart than a data warehouse. A focused data mart will get funding and gain organizational consensus a lot easier, too."
2. **Don't Worry about Integration, Keep Things Small:** "Integration can be an issue, but it has always been a problem when organizations try to take a small filing system and integrate it into an organizational system. There are always coding problems of some sort." Kramer then added, "Global systems always tend to fold, so keep it small."
3. **Spend the Extra Money if we Need help Designing our System:** Kramer commented, "Systems designing is the best place to spend the money on hiring consultants. They know the problems, and know how to deal with them. It is possible to design your own data warehouse system, but it is a lot less frustrating to hire out the design process."
4. **Keep Things Simple:** "Buy one single product from one vendor. This minimizes, or possibly eliminates any tool integration issues," Kramer advised.

5. **Be in Tune with the Users:** "Know your users," Kramer warned. "If you are not careful, you will wind up giving the right users the wrong tools, and that only leads one place - frustration. Find out who your end-users are, and work backward to the operational data. This will tell you what tools your data warehouse needs."
6. **Consider the Platforms:** Kramer said "there really are no right platforms out there. We can start with a UNIX system or Windows NT. Keep in mind that the NT has a ceiling in terms of scalability, but it works well with data marts, and most other small warehouses, just not global data warehouses."
7. **Think before Data Mine :** "Data mining is a solution in search of a problem," Kramer said. "Know what you want to find before you select the tool. Data mining software simply relieves some of the burden from the analyst."

2.4 TYPICAL OLAP OPERATIONS

- OLAP Operations (OnLine Analytical Processing Operations) refers to the act of performing actions on an OLAP system.
- The various OLAP operations are adopted in order to attain the goal of an OLAP system i.e., Decision making and Analytics from historical data.
- OLAP operations are performed over the data cubes. The concept of data cube is used because to represent the data in three or more dimensional space and so that analysts can turn around the data cube along its dimensions for all its possible space combinations to determine the every aspect of available data.
- There are five OLAP operations that can be applied over the data cube. These are Roll-up, Drill-down, Slice, Dice, Pivot (rotate).

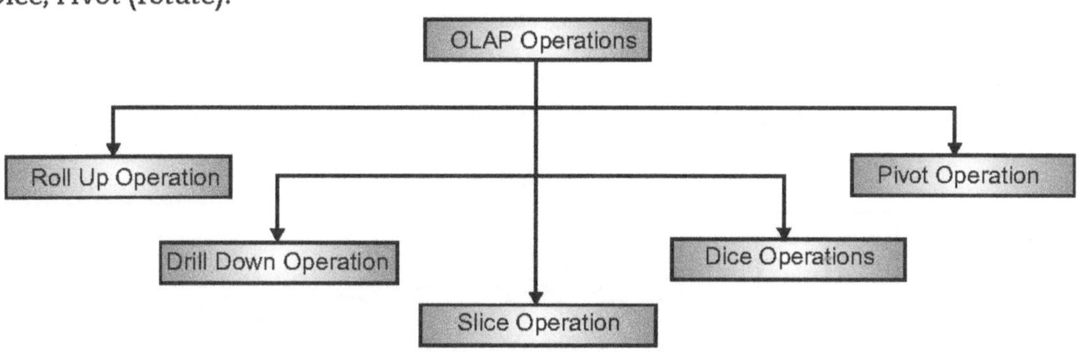

Fig. 2.8

1. Roll-up Operation:

- Roll-up is also known as "consolidation" or "aggregation." The Roll-up operation can be performed in following two ways :
  (i) Reducing dimensions
  (ii) Climbing up concept hierarchy. Concept hierarchy is a system of grouping things based on their order or level.
- Consider the Fig. 2.9. In this example, cities New jersey and Lost Angles and rolled up into country USA.
- The sales in Fig. 2.9 of New Jersey and Los Angeles are 440 and 1560 respectively. They become 2000 after roll-up.
- In this aggregation process, data is location hierarchy moves up from city to the country.
- In the roll-up process at least one or more dimensions need to be removed. In this example, Quater dimension is removed.

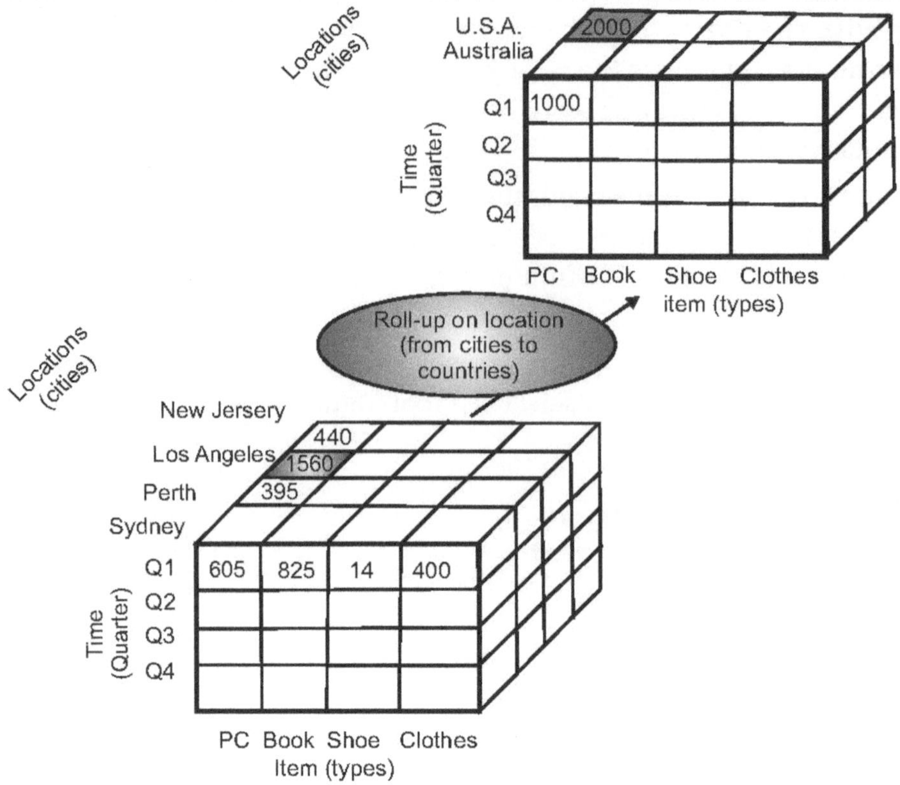

Fig. 2.9

2. **Drill operation-down:**

- In drill-down data is fragmented into smaller parts. It is the opposite of the rollup process. It can be done via
  (i) Moving down the concept hierarchy. (ii) Increasing a dimension.

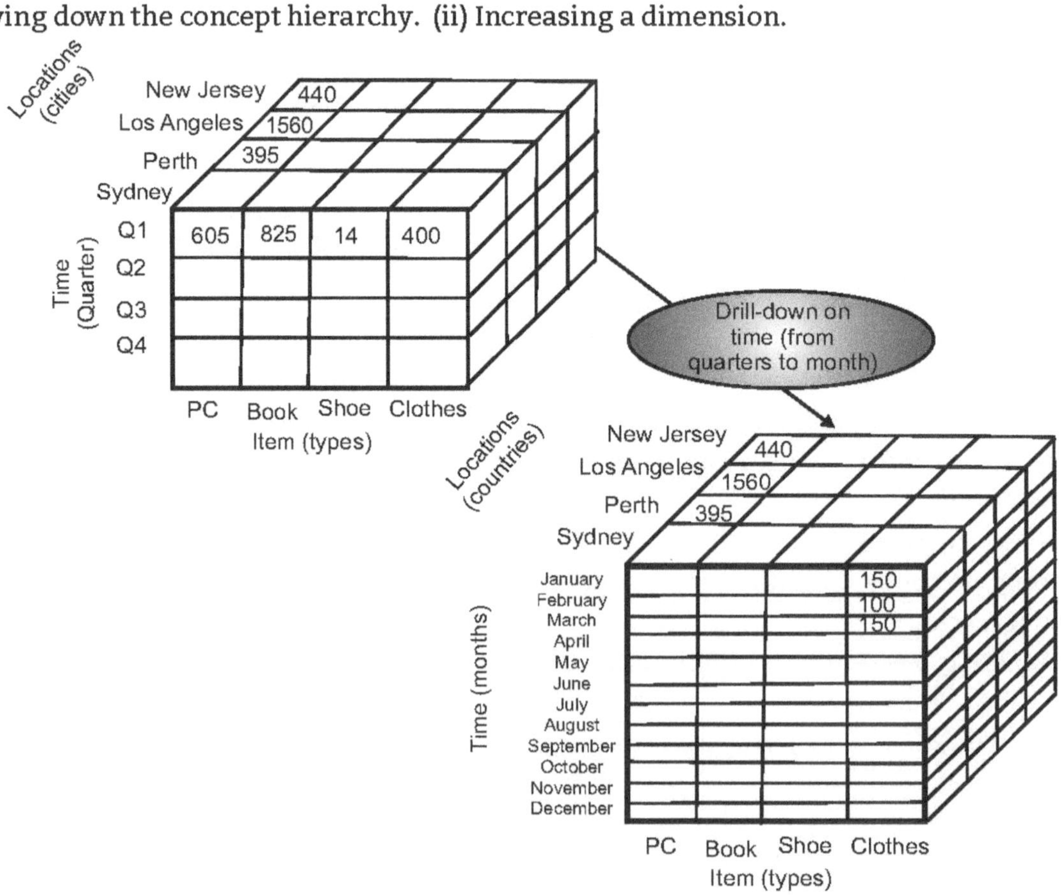

Fig. 2.10

- Consider the Fig. 2.10:
  - Quater Q1 is drilled down to months January, February, and March. Corresponding sales are also registers.
  - In this example, dimension months are added.

3. Slice Operation:

- Performing slice operation, a single dimension of the data cube can be extracted out to form a new cube. Similarly more than one dimension can also be extracted out from same data cube as required.
- Fig. 2.11 shows how slice operation performed:
  - Dimension Time is Sliced with Q1 as the filter.
  - A new cube is created altogether.

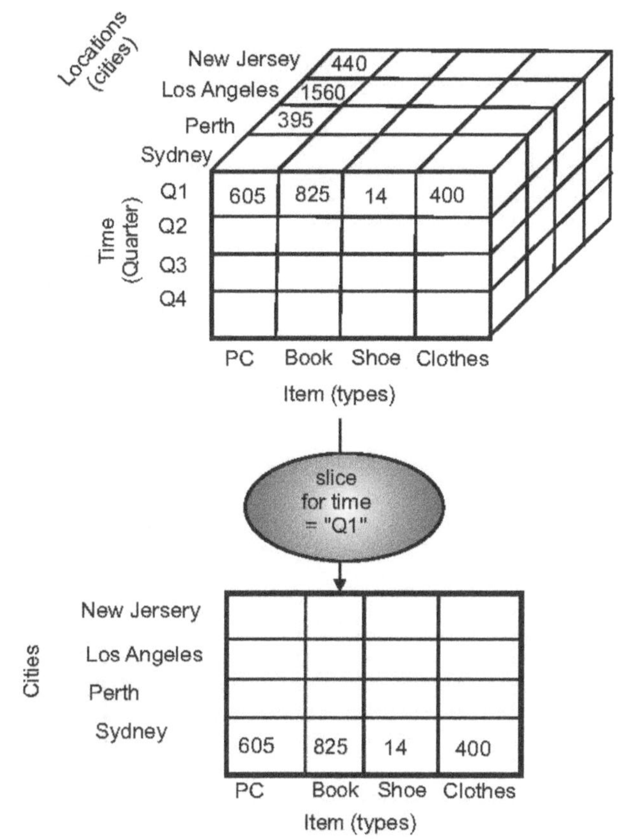

Fig. 2.11

4. Pivot Operation:

- Rotation of data cube's orientation to check for its other data views is known as pivot operation. Pivot operation provides alternate views of data available to the users.
- In the following example, the pivot is based on item types.

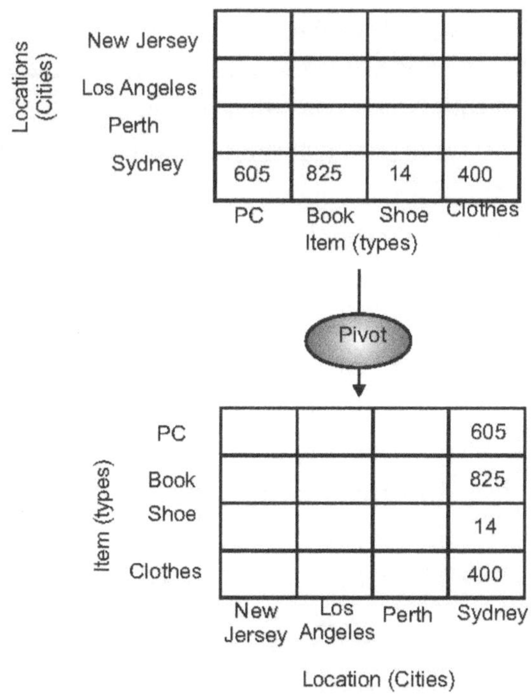

Fig. 2.12

5. Dice Operation:

- This operation is similar to a slice. Through Dice operation, a sub cube can be generated by selecting two or more than two dimension from the data cube.

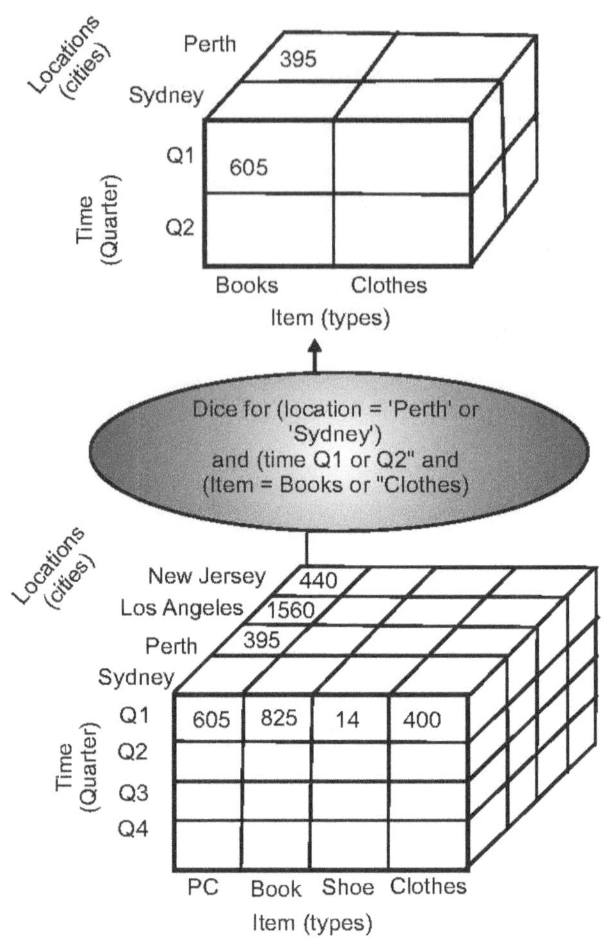

Fig. 2.13

Practice Questions

1. What is data warehousing modeling?
2. What is data warehouse model?
3. What is data cube?
4. Give difference between fact table and dimension table.
5. Explain multidimensional data model with its schemas.
6. What is OLAP? What is the need of OLAP? Explain its types.
7. Give Codd'twelve guidelines for an OLAP system.
8. Explain following operations of OLAP:
   (i) Roll up.
   (ii) Drill-down.
   (iii) Pivot.
9. Explain guidelines for OLAP.

✣ ✣ ✣

3...

Data Warehouse Designing and Online Analytical Processing II

Chapter Outcomes...

- Describe design process for the given data warehouse.
- Compare the given OLAP and OLTP tools based on the given criteria.
- Design the given data warehouse.
- Explain bitmap and join index for the given OLAP.
- Compare OLAP server Architectures for the given data warehouse.

Learning Objectives...

- To understand Basic Concepts in Data Warehouse Modeling
- To learn Process of Data Warehouse Design
- To study Business Analysis Framework for Data Warehouse
- To understand OLAP Server Architectures

3.0 INTRODUCTION

- A data warehouse is a single data repository where a record from multiple data sources is integrated for OnLine business analytical processing (OLAP).
- This implies a data warehouse needs to meet the requirements from all the business stages within the entire organization. Thus, data warehouse design is a hugely complex, lengthy, and hence error-prone process.
- Creating a data warehouse is a complex process that demands careful management, insightful leadership, adequate resources and above all, good technical design.
- The data warehouse design corresponds to a linear process in which users are indirectly implied. First, a study of the data sources and the users' analysis needs is needed. Second, the model of the data warehouse has to be built. Last the ETL (Extract Transform and Loading) process has to be defined and implemented. End users make analyses entirely driven by the data warehouse model.
- A Data Warehouse (DW) can be designed to meet users need/requirement and accommodate change in data behavior using the latest technology components such as cloud based scalable data storage for big data, real time analytics, predictive analysis and machine learning, global distribution of data, high availability, etc.

3.1 DATA WAREHOUSE DESIGN AND USAGE

- In this section, we will study data warehouse designing and its usages.

3.1.1 Data Warehouse Design

- There are a number of different possible architectures and design approaches for the development of the Data Warehouse (DW).
- The following are the typical steps involved in the data warehousing project designing:

  Step 1: Defining Business Requirements (or Requirements Gathering).

  Step 2: Setting Up Your Physical Environments.

  Step 3: Introducing Data Modeling.

  Step 4: Choosing Your Extract, Transfer, Load (ETL) Solution.

  Step 5: Online Analytic Processing (OLAP) Cube.

  Step 6: Creating the Front End.

  Step 7: Optimizing Queries.

  Step 8: Quality Assurance and Establishing a Rollout.
- Let us see above steps in detail:

1. Defining Business Requirements (or Requirements Gathering):

- Designing a data warehouse is a business-wide journey. Data warehouses touch all areas of the business, so every department needs to be on-board with the design.
- In particular, end user reporting/analysis requirements are identified, and the project team will spend the remaining period of time trying to satisfy these requirements.
- This Requirements Gathering stage should focus on the following objectives:
  (i) Aligning department goals with the overall project.
  (ii) Determining the scope of the project in relation to business objectives.
  (iii) Discovering our future needs and current needs by diving deep into our data (find out what data will be useful for analysis) and our current tech stack (where your data is currently siloed / not being put to use?).
  (iv) Creating a disaster recovery plan in the case of system failure.
  (v) Thinking about each layer of security (e.g., threat detection, threat mitigation, identity controls, monitoring, risk reduction, etc.).
  (vi) Anticipating compliance needs and mitigating regulatory risks.

2. Setting Up the Physical Environments:

- Data warehouses typically have three primary physical environments-development, testing, and production. At a minimum, there should be separate physical application and database servers as well as separate ETL/ELT, OLAP, cube, and reporting processes set up for development, testing, and production.
- Building separate physical environments ensure that all changes can be tested before moving them to production, development, and testing can occur without halting the production environment and if data integrity becomes suspect, the IT staff can investigate the issue without negatively impacting the production environment.

3. Introducing Data Modeling:

- Data modeling is the process of visualizing data distribution in our warehouse. Before are start building a house, we want to know what goes where and why it goes there. That is what data modeling is to data warehouses.
- Data modeling helps to visualize the relationships between data, and it's useful for setting standardized naming conventions, creating relationships between data sets, and establishing compliance and security processes that align with your overarching IT goals.
- The three most popular data models for warehouses are Snowflake Schema, Star Schema and Galaxy Schema.
- Part of the data modeling exercise is often the identification of data sources. Sometimes this step is deferred until the ETL step.

4. Choosing the Extract, Transfer, Load (ETL) Solution:

- The ETL (Extraction, Transformation, Loading) process typically takes the longest to develop, and this can easily take up to 50% of the data warehouse implementation cycle or longer.
- The reason for this is that it takes time to get the source data, understand the necessary columns, understand the business rules, and understand the logical and physical data models.

5. Online Analytic Processing (OLAP) Cube:

- A data warehouse is where we are storing the business data in an easily analyzable format to be used for a variety of business needs.
- Online analytical processing cubes help us to analyze the data in the data warehouse or data mart. Most of the time, OLAP cubes are used for reporting, but they have plenty of other use cases.
- Since the data warehouse will have data coming in from multiple data pipelines, OLAP cubes help us to organize all of that data in a multi-dimensional format that makes analyzing it rapid and straightforward.
- The three critical elements of OLAP design include:
  - **(i) Grouping measures** - numerical values you want to analyze such as revenue, number of customers, how many products customers purchase, or average purchase amount.
  - **(ii) Dimension** - where measures are stored for analysis such as geographic region, month, or quarter.
  - **(iii) Granularity** - the lowest level of detail that you want to include in the OLAP dataset.

6. Creating the Front End:

- The next step is to work on how users will access the data warehouse. Front end development is how users will access the data for analysis and run reports.
- There are many options available, including building your front end in-house or purchasing an off the shelf product.

7. Optimizing Queries:

- For any production database, SQL query performance becomes an issue sooner or later. Having long-running queries not only consumes system resources that makes the server and application run slowly, but also may lead to table locking and data corruption issues.
- So, query optimization becomes an important task. Following are several specific query optimization strategies one can use:
  - **(i) Use Index:** Using an index is the first strategy one should use to speed up a query.
  - **(ii) Aggregate Table:** Pre-populating tables at higher levels so less amount of data need to be parsed.

(iii) **Vertical Partitioning:** Partition the table by columns. This strategy decreases the amount of data a SQL query needs to process.

(iv) **Horizontal Partitioning:** Partition the table by data value, most often time. This strategy decreases the amount of data a SQL query needs to process.

(v) **Denormalization:** The process of denormalization combines multiple tables into a single table. This speeds up query performance because fewer table joins are needed.

(vi) **Server Tuning:** Each server has its own parameters, and often tuning server parameters so that it can fully take advantage of the hardware resources can significantly speed up query performance.

8. Quality Assurance and Establishing a Rollout:

- Once, the development team declares that everything is ready for further testing, the QA team takes over. The QA team is always from the client. Usually the QA team members will know little about data warehousing.
- Once, the QA team completes quality assurance then it is time for the data warehouse system to go live. It's also the time to start thinking about education, training, and use cases.

3.1.2 Usage of Data Warehouse

- Data warehouses are widely used in the following fields:

1. Banking:

- In the banking industry, concentration is given to risk management and policy reversal as well analyzing consumer data, market trends, government regulations and reports, and more importantly financial decision making.
- Most banks also use warehouses to manage the resources available on deck in an effective manner. Certain banking sectors utilize them for market research, performance analysis of each product, interchange and exchange rates, and to develop marketing programs.
- Analysis of card holder's transactions, spending patterns and merchant classification, all of which provide the bank with an opportunity to introduce special offers and lucrative deals based on cardholder activity. Apart from all these, there is also scope for co-branding.

2. Hospitality:

- A major proportion of this industry is dominated by hotel and restaurant services, car rental services, and holiday home services.
- They utilize warehouse services to design and evaluate their advertising and promotion campaigns where they target customers based on their feedback and travel patterns.

3. Finance:

- Similar to the applications seen in banking, mainly revolve around evaluation and trends of customer expenses which aids in maximizing the profits earned by their clients.

4. Transportation Industry:

- In the transportation industry, data warehouses record customer data enabling traders to experiment with target marketing where the marketing campaigns are designed by keeping customer requirements in mind.
- The internal environment of the industry uses them to analyze customer feedback, performance, manage crews on board as well as analyze customer financial reports for pricing strategies.

5. Government and Education:

- The government uses data warehouses to maintain and analyze tax records, health policy records and their respective providers, and also their entire criminal law database is connected to the state's data warehouse.

- Criminal activity is predicted from the patterns and trends, results of the analysis of historical data associated with past criminals.
- Universities use warehouses for extracting of information used for the proposal of research grants, understanding their student demographics, and human resource management.
- The entire financial department of most universities depends on data warehouses, inclusive of the Financial Aid department.

6. Service Sectors:

- Data warehouses find themselves to be of use in the service sector for maintenance of financial records, revenue patterns, customer profiling, resource management, and human resources.

7. Telephone Industry:

- The telephone industry operates over both offline and online data burdening them with a lot of historical data which has to be consolidated and integrated.
- Apart from those operations, analysis of fixed assets, analysis of customer's calling patterns for sales representatives to push advertising campaigns, and tracking of customer queries, all require the facilities of a data warehouse.

8. Manufacturing and Distribution Industry:

- A manufacturing organization has to take several make-or-buy decisions which can influence the future of the sector, which is why they utilize high-end OLAP tools as a part of data warehouses to predict market changes, analyze current business trends, detect warning conditions, view marketing developments, and ultimately take better decisions.
- They also use them for product shipment records, records of product portfolios, identify profitable product lines, analyze previous data and customer feedback to evaluate the weaker product lines and eliminate them.
- For the distributions, the supply chain management of products operates through data warehouses.

9. Healthcare:

- One of the most important sector which utilizes data warehouses is the Healthcare sector.
- All of their financial, clinical, and employee records are fed to warehouses as it helps them to strategize and predict outcomes, track and analyze their service feedback, generate patient reports, share data with tie-in insurance companies, medical aid services, etc.

Benefits of Data Warehouse Usage:

1. **Improved Control of Data:** Information in the data warehouse is under the control of data warehouse users so that, even if the source system data is removed over time, the information in the warehouse can be stored safely for extended periods of time.
2. **Better Retrieval of Data:** Because they are separate from operational systems, data warehouses provide retrieval of data without slowing down operational systems.
3. **Increased Productivity of Corporate Decision Makers:** Data warehousing improves the productivity of corporate decision makers by creating an integrated database of consistent, subject-oriented, historical data. It integrates data from multiple incompatible systems into a form that provides one consistent view of the organization. By transforming data into meaningful information, a data warehouse allows business managers to perform more substantive, accurate, and consistent analysis.
4. **More Cost-Effective Decision-Making:** Data warehousing helps to reduce the overall cost of the product by reducing the number of channels.

5. **Better Enterprise Intelligence:** It helps to provide better enterprise intelligence and enhanced customer service.
6. **Potential High Returns on Investment:** Return On Investment (ROI) refers to the amount of increased revenue. Implementations of data warehouses and complementary business intelligence systems have enabled business to generate higher amounts of revenue and provide substantial cost savings.
7. **Competitive Advantage:** The huge returns on investment for those companies/organizations that have successfully implemented a data warehouse is evidence of the enormous competitive advantage that accompanies this technology. The competitive advantage is gained by allowing decision-makers access to data that can reveal previously unavailable, unknown, and untapped information on, for example, customers, trends, and demands.

3.2 A BUSINESS ANALYSIS FRAMEWORK FOR DATA WAREHOUSE DESIGN

- In this section first we will discuss the advantages or benefits to business analyst from a data warehouse. Following are the points which highlight the benefits to business analysts from data warehouse:
  1. A data warehouse provide a **competitive advantage** by presenting relevant information from which to measure performance and make critical adjustments to help win over competitors.
  2. A data warehouse can enhance business **productivity** because it is able to quickly and efficiently gather information that accurately describes the organization.
  3. A data warehouse facilitates **customer relationship management** because it provides a consistent view of customers and items across all lines of business, all departments, and all markets.
  4. A data warehouse may bring about **cost reduction** by tracking trends, patterns, and exceptions over long periods in a consistent and reliable manner.
- To design an effective data warehouse we need to understand and analyze business needs and construct a business analysis framework.
- The construction of data warehouse can be viewed as the construction of a large and complex building, for which the owner, architect, and builder have different views.
- Four different views regarding a data warehouse design must be considered:
  1. The **top-down view** allows the selection of the relevant information necessary for the data warehouse. This information matches current and future business needs.
  2. The **data source view** exposes the information being captured, stored, and managed by operational systems. This information may be documented at various levels of detail and accuracy, from individual data source tables to integrated data source tables. Data sources are often modeled by traditional data modeling techniques, such as the entity-relationship model or CASE (Computer-Aided Software Engineering) tools.
  3. The **data warehouse view** includes fact tables and dimension tables. It represents the information that is stored inside the data warehouse, including pre-calculated totals and counts, as well as information regarding the source, date, and time of origin, added to provide historical context.
  4. Finally, the **business query view** is the data perspective in the data warehouse from the end-user's view.

- Building and using a data warehouse is a complex task because it requires following skills:
    1. **Business skills** are required for building a data warehouse involves understanding how systems store and manage their data, using a data warehouse involves understanding the significance of the data it contains, as well as understanding and translating the business requirements into queries that can be satisfied by the data warehouse.
    2. **Technology skills** involve the ability to discover patterns and trends, to extrapolate trends based on history and look for rare events, and to present relevant recommendations based on such analysis.
    3. **Program management** *skills* involve the need to interface with many technologies, vendors, and end-users in order to deliver results in a timely and cost-effective manner.

3.3 DATA WAREHOUSE DESIGN PROCESS

- A data warehouse can be built using a top-down approach, a bottom-up approach, or a combination of both.
    1. The **top-down approach** starts with overall design and planning. It is useful in cases where the technology is mature and well known, and where the business problems that must be solved are clear and well understood.
    2. The **bottom-up approach** starts with experiments and prototypes. This is useful in the early stage of business modeling and technology development. It allows an organization to move forward at considerably less expense and to evaluate the technological benefits before making significant commitments.
    3. In the **combined approach**, an organization can exploit the planned and strategic nature of the top-down approach while retaining the rapid implementation and opportunistic application of the bottom-up approach.
- From the software engineering point of view, the design and construction of a data warehouse may consist of the following steps:

    Step 1: Defining Business Requirements (or Requirements Gathering).

    Step 2: Setting Up Your Physical Environments.

    Step 3: Introducing Data Modeling.

    Step 4: Choosing Your Extract, Transfer, Load (ETL) Solution.

    Step 5: Online Analytic Processing (OLAP) Cube.

    Step 6: Creating the Front End.

    Step 7: Optimizing Queries.

    Step 8: Quality Assurance and Establishing a Rollout.
- Detail of all these steps are given in Section 3.1.1 of this chapter.
- Large software systems can be developed using one of two methodologies:
    1. The **waterfall method** performs a structured and systematic analysis at each step before proceeding to the next, which is like a waterfall, falling from one step to the next.
    2. The **spiral method** involves the rapid generation of increasingly functional systems, with short intervals between successive releases. This is considered a good choice for data warehouse development, especially for data marts, because the turnaround time is short, modifications can be done quickly, and new designs and technologies can be adapted in a timely manner.

- In general, the **warehouse design process** consists of the following steps:
  1. Choose **a business process** to model. If the business process is organizational and involves multiple complex object collections, a data warehouse model should be followed. However, if the process is departmental and focuses on the analysis of one kind of business process, a data mart model should be chosen.
  2. Choose the business process **grain**, which is the fundamental, atomic level of data to be represented in the fact table for this process. For example, individual transactions, individual daily record.
  3. Choose the **dimensions** that will apply to each fact table record. For example, time, item, customer, supplier, warehouse, transaction type, and status.
  4. Choose the **measures** that will populate each fact table record. For example, dollars sold and units sold.
- In addition to above there are various points need to take care while at the time of warehouse design:
  1. Data warehouse implementation scope should be clearly defined. The goals of data warehouse implementation should be **specific, achievable,** and **measurable** which involves determining the time and budget allocations.
  2. Once a data warehouse is designed and constructed, the **initial deployment of the warehouse, platform upgrades and maintenance** must also be considered.
  3. Scope management should be considered which includes **controlling the number and range of queries, dimensions, and reports; limiting the data warehouse's size; or limiting the schedule, budget, or resources.**
- A recommended method for the development of data warehouse systems is to implement the warehouse in an incremental and evolutionary manner, as shown in Fig. 3.1.

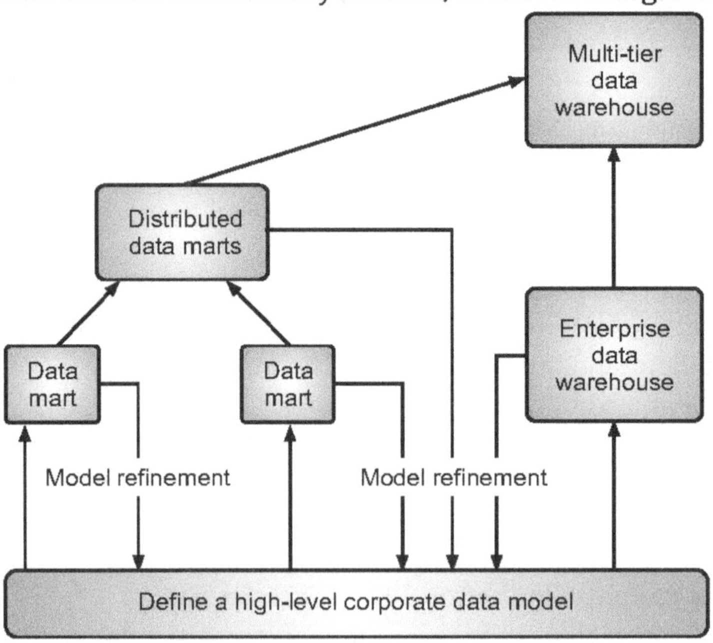

Fig. 3.1 : A Recommended Approach for Data Warehouse Development

- First, a high-level corporate data model is defined within a reasonably short period of time (such as one or two months) that provides a corporate-wide, consistent, integrated view of data among different subjects and potential usages.
- This high-level model, although it will need to be refined in the further development of enterprise data warehouses and departmental data marts, will greatly reduce future integration problems.

- Second, independent data marts can be implemented in parallel with the enterprise warehouse based on the same corporate data model set as above.
- Third, distributed data marts can be constructed to integrate different data marts via hub servers.
- Finally, a multitier data warehouse is constructed where the enterprise warehouse is the sole custodian of all warehouse data, which is then distributed to the various dependent data marts.

3.4 DATA WAREHOUSE USEAGE FOR INFORMATION PROCESSING

- Data warehouses and data marts are used in a wide range of applications. Business executives use the data in data warehouses and data marts to perform data analysis and make strategic decisions.
- The evolution of data warehouse takes place throughout a number of phases. Some of them are explained below:
  1. Initially, the data warehouse is used for generating reports and answering predefined queries with help of **access** and **retrieval tools.**
  2. Progressively, it is used to analyze summarized and detailed data, where the results are presented in the form of reports and charts with help of database **reporting tools.**
  3. Later, the data warehouse is used for strategic purposes, performing multidimensional analysis and sophisticated slice-and-dice operations with help of **data analysis tools.**
  4. Finally, the data warehouse is employed for knowledge discovery and strategic decision making using **data mining tools.**
- Business users need to have the means to know what exists in the data warehouse (through metadata), how to access the contents of the data warehouse, how to examine the contents using analysis tools, and how to present the results of such analysis.
- There are three kinds of data warehouse applications namely, information processing, analytical processing, and data mining.
  1. **Information processing** supports querying, basic statistical analysis, and reporting using crosstabs, tables, charts or graphs. A current trend in data warehouse information processing is to construct low-cost web-based accessing tools that are then integrated with web browsers.
  2. **Analytical processing** supports basic OLAP operations, including slice-and-dice, drill-down, roll-up, and pivoting. It generally operates on historic data in both summarized and detailed forms. The major strength of online analytical processing over information processing is the multidimensional data analysis of data warehouse data.
  3. **Data mining** supports knowledge discovery by finding hidden patterns and associations, constructing analytical models, performing classification and prediction, and presenting the mining results using visualization tools.
- Information processing, based on queries, can find useful information. However, answers to such queries reflect the information directly stored in databases or computable by aggregate functions. They do not reflect sophisticated patterns or regularities buried in the database.
- Therefore, information processing is not data mining but Analytic Processing and data mining make use of information processing to achieve their objectives.

Difference between Analytical Processing and Data Mining:

Sr. No.	Analytical Processing	Data Mining
1.	OLAP is a data summarization/aggregation tool that helps simplify data analysis.	Data mining allows the automated discovery of implicit patterns and interesting knowledge hidden in large amounts of data.
2.	OLAP tools are targeted toward simplifying and supporting interactive data analysis.	The goal of data mining tools is to automate as much of the process as possible, while still allowing users to guide the process. In this sense, data mining goes one step beyond traditional online analytical processing.
3.	OLAP systems can present general descriptions of data from data warehouses.	Data mining covers a much broader spectrum than simple OLAP operations.
4.	OLAP functions are data summarization and comparison (by drilling, pivoting, slicing, dicing, and other operations).	Data mining performs not only data summarization and comparison but also association, classification, prediction, clustering, time-series analysis, and other data analysis tasks.
5.	OLAP systems have limited applications as compare to data mining.	Data mining involves more automated and deeper analysis than OLAP, hence have broader applications.

3.4.1 From OLAP to Multidimensional Data Mining

- In the domain of data mining, significant research has been taken place for data mining on various platforms like transaction databases, relational databases, spatial databases, text databases, time-series databases, flat files, data warehouses, and so on.
- OnLine Analytical Mining (OLAM) also called OLAP mining integrates OnLine Analytical Processing (OLAP) with data mining and mining knowledge in multidimensional databases.
- In simple words, we can say that OLAM is integration of data warehouse and data mining. Following points discuss the importance of OLAM:
  1. **Fast Mining Response:** Integration of OnLine analytical processing (OLAP) with data mining provide quick/fast response to user queries.
  2. **High Quality of Data in Data Warehouses**: A data warehouse constructed by certain pre-processing (cleaning, integration and transformation) serves as a valuable source of high quality data for OLAP as well as for data mining. OLAM can make use of this integrated, consistent and clean data.
  3. **Availability of Infrastructure Surrounding Data Warehouses:** Data warehouse provide information processing and data analysis infrastructures which include accessing, integration, consolidation, and transformation of multiple heterogeneous databases, ODBC/OLEDB connections, Web-accessing and service facilities, and reporting and OLAP analysis tools. Availability of such infrastructures make it simple to use its functionalities instead of creating from scratch.

4. **OLAP Based Exploratory Data Analysis:** OnLine analytical mining provides pivoting, drilling, dicing and slicing provides capability to mine data on different data subsets and abstraction levels. This, together with data/knowledge visualization tools, will greatly enhance the power and flexibility of exploratory data mining.
5. **OnLine Selection of Data Mining Functions:** By integrating OLAP with multiple data mining functions, OLAM allows choosing the right data mining functions and dynamically change their data mining tasks.

3.5 DATA WAREHOUSE IMPLEMENTATION

- Data warehouses contain huge amount of data which is processes and analysed by OLAP server. OLAP servers require that decision support queries should be answered in the order of seconds.
- Therefore, it is crucial for data warehouse systems to support highly efficient cube computation techniques, access methods, and query processing techniques.

3.5.1 Efficient Data Cube Computation (An Overview)

- At the core of multidimensional data analysis is the efficient computation of aggregations across many sets of dimensions.
- In SQL terms, these aggregations are referred to as group-by's. Each group-by can be represented by a cuboid, where the set of group-by's forms a lattice of cuboids defining a data cube. In this subsection, we explore issues relating to the efficient computation of data cubes.

Compute Cube Operator:

- One approach to cube computation extends SQL so as to include a compute cube operator. It computes the aggregates over all subsets of the dimensions specified in the operation. This can require excessive storage space, especially for large numbers of dimensions

Syntax:

```
compute cube  cube_name
```

Example 1: Suppose that we want to create a data cube for "Sales" that contains city, item, year, and sales in dollars. Here city, item, and year are the dimensions and sales in dollars is the fact/measure of data cube. What is the total number of cuboids, or group-by's, that can be computed for this data cube?

For a cube with n dimensions, there are a total of 2^n cuboids, including the base cuboid. The total number of cuboids depends on total no. of dimensions and can be computed for this data cube is $2^3 = 8$.

The possible group-by's are {(city, item, year), (city, item), (city, year), (item, year), (city), (item), (year), ()} where () means that the group-by is empty. These group-by's form a lattice of cuboids for the data cube, as shown in Fig. 3.2.

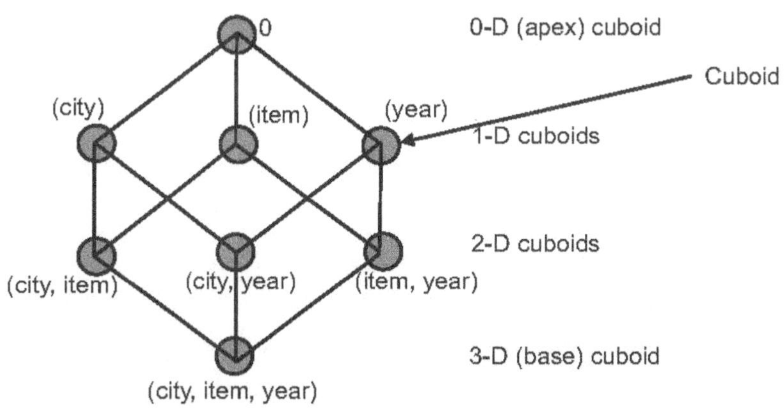

Fig. 3.2

- The base cuboid contains all three dimensions, city, item, and year. It can return the total sales for any combination of the three dimensions.
- The base cuboid is the least generalized (most specific) of the cuboids. A cell in the base cuboid is a base cell. A cell from a nonbase cuboid is an aggregate cell.
- The apex cuboid, or 0-D cuboid, refers to the case where the group-by is empty. It contains the total sum of all sales. The apex cuboid is the most generalized (least specific) of the cuboids, and is often denoted as all.
- If we start at the apex cuboid and explore downward in the lattice, this is equivalent to drilling down within the data cube. If we start at the base cuboid and explore upward, this is akin to rolling up.

Example 2: On Data cube "Sales" we want to analyze data with following queries:

Query 1: "Compute the sum of sales."

Query 2: "Compute the sum of sales, grouping by city."

Query 3: "Compute the sum of sales, grouping by city and item."

- Here, Query 1 containing no group-by constraint is a zero dimensional operation and get data at apex (0-D) cuboid in data cube. Query 2 containing one group-by constraint is a one-dimensional operation and gets data at 1-D cuboid level in data cube. Query 3 is a two-dimensional operation and get data at 2-D cuboid level in data cube. A cube operator on n dimensions is equivalent to a collection of group-by statements, one for each subset of the n dimensions. Therefore, the cube operator is the n-dimensional generalization of the group-by operator. Online analytical processing may need to access different cuboids for different queries. Therefore, it is good to compute in advance all or at least some of the cuboids in a data cube which leads to fast response time and avoids some redundant computation.
- Similar to the SQL syntax, the data cube in this example, could be defined as define cube,

  Sales cube [city, item, year]: sum(sales in dollars)
- In the example, a cube having 3 dimensions hence, there will be total of 8 cuboids. A statement such as compute cube sales cube would explicitly instruct the system to compute the Sales aggregate cuboids for all eight subsets of the set {city, item, year}, including the empty subset.

Curse of Dimensionality:

- As discussed earlier, it is good to compute in advance all or at least some of the cuboids in a data cube which leads to fast response time and avoids some redundant computation.
- But the challenge associated with this pre-computation is that required storage space may explode if the cube has many dimensions.
- The storage requirements are even more excessive when many of the dimensions have associated concept hierarchies, each with multiple levels. This problem is referred to as the curse of dimensionality.
- As we already illustrated that if there are no hierarchies associated with each dimension, then for a cube with n dimensions, there are a total of 2^n cuboids, including the base cuboid. However, in real time, many dimensions do have hierarchies.
- For example, time is usually explored not at only one conceptual level (e.g., year), but rather at multiple conceptual levels such as in the hierarchy "day <month < quarter < year."
- For an n-dimensional data cube, the total number of cuboids that can be generated (including the cuboids generated by climbing up the hierarchies along each dimension) is,

$$\text{Total number of cuboids} = \prod_{i=1}^{n} (L_i + 1) \qquad ...(3.1)$$

Where L_i is the number of levels associated with dimension i. One is added to L_i in eq. (3.1) to include the virtual top level, all, (generalizing to all is equivalent to the removal of the dimension).

- If the cube has 10 dimensions and each dimension has five levels (virtual level all), the total number of cuboids that can be generated is $5^{10} \approx 9.8 \times 10^6$.
- As the number of dimensions, number of conceptual hierarchies (cardinality) increases, the storage space required for many of the group-by's will grossly exceed the (fixed) size of the input relation.
- Now, it is clear that it is unrealistic to precompute and materialize all of the cuboids. If there are many cuboids and these cuboids are large in size, a more reasonable option is partial materialization; i.e., to materialize only some of the possible cuboids that can be generated.

Partial Materialization: Selected Computation of Cuboids:

- There are three choices for data cube materialization given a base cuboid:
  1. **No Materialization:** Do not precompute any of the cuboids. This leads to computing expensive multidimensional aggregates on-the-fly, which can be extremely slow.
  2. **Full Materialization:** Precompute all of the cuboids. The resulting lattice of computed cuboids is referred to as the full cube. This choice typically requires huge amounts of memory space in order to store all of the precomputed cuboids.
  3. **Partial Materialization:** One approach is to selectively compute a proper subset of the whole set of possible cuboids. Alternatively approach is called subcube where only some of the cells may be precomputed for various cuboids based on some user-specified criterion, such as where the tuple count of each cell is above some threshold.
- Partial materialization represents an interesting trade-off between storage space and response time. The partial materialization of cuboids or subcubes should consider three factors:
  1. Identify the subset of cuboids or subcubes to materialize;
  2. Exploit the materialized cuboids or subcubes during query processing; and
  3. Efficiently update the materialized cuboids or subcubes during load and refresh.
- The selection of the subset of cuboids or subcubes to materialize should take into account:
  - The queries in the workload, their frequencies, and their accessing costs.
  - Workload characteristics, the cost for incremental updates, and the total storage requirements.
  - Physical database design such as the generation and selection of indices.
- Few approaches which are used for cuboid and subcube selection are:
  - Several OLAP products have adopted **heuristic approaches for cuboid** and **subcube selection**. A popular approach is to materialize the cuboids set on which other frequently referenced cuboids are based.
  - Alternatively, we can compute an **iceberg cube**, which is a data cube that stores only those cube cells with an aggregate value (e.g., count) that is above some minimum support threshold.
  - Another common strategy is to materialize a **shell cube**. This involves precomputing the cuboids for only a small number of dimensions (e.g., three to five) of a data cube. Queries on additional combinations of the dimensions can be computed on-the-fly.
- Once, the selected cuboids have been materialized by using one of above approaches, it is important to take advantage of them during query processing. This involves several issues, as given below:
  1. How to determine the relevant cuboid(s) from among the candidate materialized cuboids?
  2. How to use available index structures on the materialized cuboids?
  3. How to transform the OLAP operations onto the selected cuboid(s)?
- Finally, during load and refresh, the materialized cuboids should be updated efficiently.

3.6 INDEXING OLAP DATA (BITMAP INDEX AND JOIN INDEX)

- Most data warehouse systems support index structures and materialized views (using cuboids) to facilitate efficient data accessing. We have already studied the materialized views in previous section.
- Here, we will discuss the index structures use in data warehouse.

3.6.1 Bitmap Indexing

- The bitmap indexing method is popular in OLAP products because it allows quick searching in data cubes. A bitmap index is a specialized variation of a B-tree index.
- The advantages of using bitmap indexes are greatest for low cardinality columns i.e., columns in which the number of distinct values is small compared to the number of rows in the table.
- A gender column, which only has two distinct values (male and female), is ideal for a bitmap index. The data warehouse administrators also build bitmap indexes on columns with higher cardinalities.
- The bitmap index is an alternative representation of the Record ID (RID) list. In the bitmap index for a given attribute, there is a distinct bit vector, B_v, for each value v in the attribute's domain.
- If a given attribute's domain consists of n values, then n bits are needed for each entry in the bitmap index (i.e., there are n bit vectors).
- If the attribute has the value v for a given row in the data table, then the bit representing that value is set to 1 in the corresponding row of the bitmap index. All other bits for that row are set to 0.

Example: Assume that the column for color has three distinct colors, namely, white, almond and black. Construct a bitmap using these three distinct values. Each entry in the bitmap contains three bits. Let us say the first bit refers to white, the second to almond, and the third to black. If a product is white in color, the bitmap entry for that product consists of three bits i.e. 100, where the first bit is set to 1, the second bit is set to 0, and the third bit is set to 0. If a product is almond in color, the bitmap entry for that product consists of three bits i.e. 010, where the first bit is set to 0, the second bit is set to 1, and the third bit is set to 0.

Extract of Sales Data:

Address or Rowid	Date	Product	Color	Region	Sales (S)
00001BFE.0012.0111	15-Nov-00	Dishwasher	White	East	300
00001BFE.0013.0114	15-Nov-00	Dryer	Almond	West	450
00001BFF.0012.0115	16-Nov-00	Dishwasher	Almond	West	350
00001BFF.0012.0138	16-Nov-00	Washer	Black	North	550
00001BFF.0012.0145	17-Nov-00	Washer	White	South	500
00001BFF.0012.0157	17-Nov-00	Dryer	White	East	400
00001BFF.0014.0165	17-Nov-00	Washer	Almond	South	575

Bitmapped Index for Product Column
Ordered bits: Washer, Dryer, Dishwasher

Address or Rowid	Bitmap
00001BFE.0012.0111	001
00001BFE.0013.0114	010
00001BFF.0012.0115	001
00001BFF.0012.0138	100
00001BFF.0012.0145	100
00001BFF.0012.0157	010
00001BFF.0014.0165	100

Bitmapped Index for Color Column
Ordered bits: White, Almond, Black

Address or Rowid	Bitmap
00001BFE.0012.0111	100
00001BFE.0013.0114	010
00001BFF.0012.0115	010
00001BFF.0012.0138	001
00001BFF.0012.0145	100
00001BFF.0012.0157	100
00001BFF.0014.0165	010

Bitmapped Index for Region Column
Ordered bits: East, West, North South

Address or Rowid	Bitmap
00001BFE.0012.0111	1000
00001BFE.0013.0114	0100
00001BFF.0012.0115	0100
00001BFF.0012.0138	0010
00001BFF.0012.0145	0001
00001BFF.0012.0157	1000
00001BFF.0014.0165	0001

Fig. 3.3 : Bitmapped Index Example

- How do the bitmapped indexes work to retrieve the requested rows? Consider a query against the Sales table in the above example:

```
SELECT rows FROM Sales TABLE WHERE Product IS "Washer" AND Color IS "Almond"
                                                    AND Division IS "East" OR "South"
```

- Fig. 3.4 illustrates how Boolean logic is applied to find the result set based on the bitmapped indexes shown in Fig. 3.3.

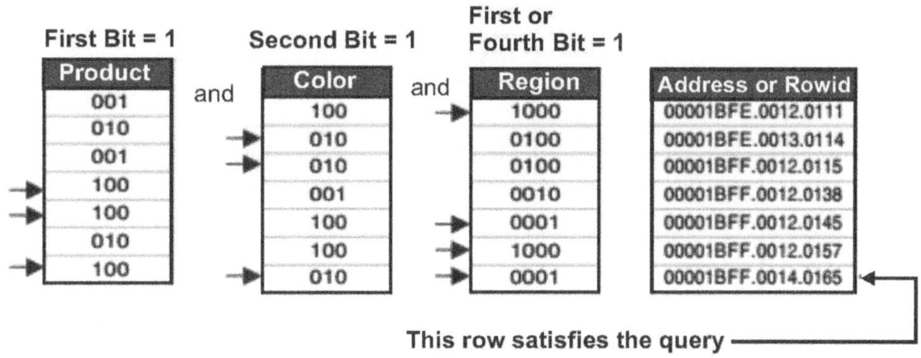

Fig. 3.4 : Bitmapped Indexes (Data Retrieval)

- Bitmap indexes are widely used in data warehousing environments where the environments typically have large amounts of data and ad hoc queries.
- Bitmap indexing is advantageous compared to other indexing techniques. Some of these are given below:
  1. Reduced response time for large classes of ad hoc queries.
  2. It is useful for low-cardinality domains because comparison, join, and aggregation operations are then reduced to bit arithmetic, which substantially reduces the processing time.
  3. For higher-cardinality domains, the method can be adapted using compression techniques.
  4. Reduced storage requirements compared to other indexing techniques. Bitmap indexing leads to significant reductions in space and Input/Output (I/O) since, a string of characters can be represented by a single bit.
  5. Dramatic performance gains even on hardware with a relatively small number of CPUs or a small amount of memory.
  6. Efficient maintenance during parallel DML and loads.

3.6.2 Joint Indexing

- The join indexing method gained popularity from its use in relational database query processing.
- Traditional indexing maps the value in a given column to a list of rows having that value. In contrast, join indexing registers the joinable rows of two relations from a relational database.
- Let R and S be two relations, not necessarily distinct. We consider two relations R(RID, A) and S (B, SID) join on the attributes A and B, then the join index record contains the pair (RID, SID) where RID and SID are record identifiers from the R and S relations, respectively.
- A join index is an abstraction of the join of the two relations. Hence, the join index records can identify joinable tuples without performing costly join operations.
- The purpose of a join index is to accelerate common joins, even equijoins. One of the advantages of join indices is that they can be represented in a very compact way, allowing for highly efficient access.
- For example, suppose that the DBMS is to evaluate a query,

```
"SELECT R.A. FROM R,S WHERE R.A = S.B."
```

- A conventional join would use a nested loop algorithm, with an indexed scan in the inner loop. With a join index, the join can be computed by scanning the join index, thus minimizing random I/O.

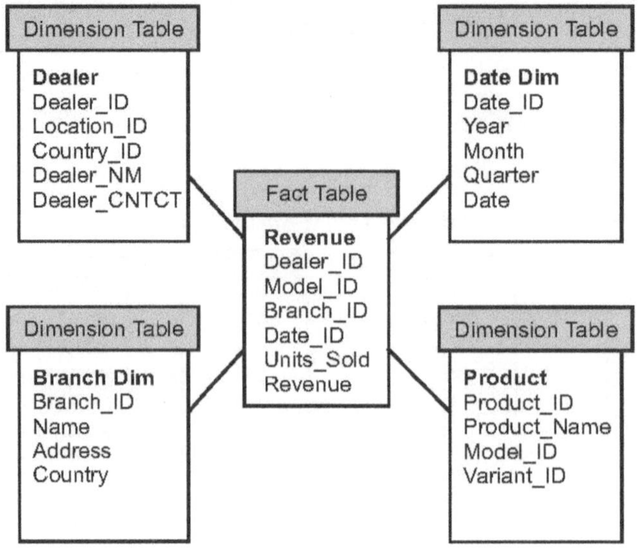

Fig. 3.5

- Join indexing is especially useful for maintaining the relationship between a foreign key and its matching primary keys, from the joinable relation.
- The star schema model of data warehouses makes join indexing attractive for crosstable search, because the linkage between a fact table and its corresponding dimension tables comprises the fact table's foreign key and the dimension table's primary key.
- Join indexing maintains relationships between attribute values of a dimension (e.g., within a dimension table) and the corresponding rows in the fact table.
- Join indices may span multiple dimensions to form composite join indices. We can use join indices to identify subcubes that are of interest.

Example 1: An example of a join index relationship between the sales fact table and the location and item dimension tables is shown in Fig. 3.6. For example,

(i) The "Main Street" value in the location dimension table joins with tuples T57, T238, and T884 of the sales fact table.

(ii) Similarly, the "Sony-TV" value in the item dimension table joins with tuples T57 and T459 of the sales fact table.

The corresponding join index tables are shown in Fig. 3.7.

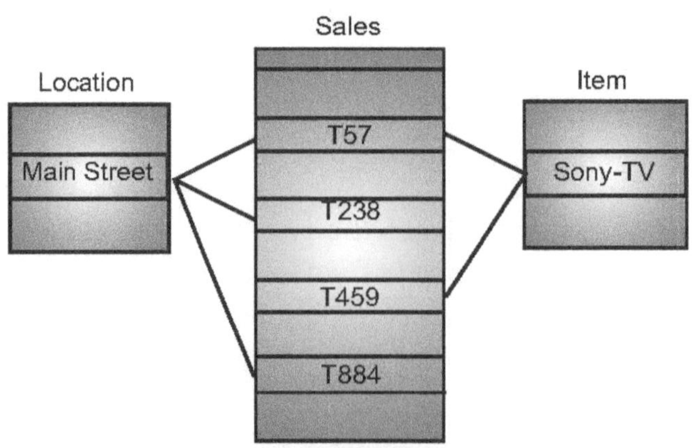

Fig. 3.6 : Linkages between a sales fact table and location and item dimension tables

Join index table for Locational/sales

Location	Sales Key
Main Street	T57
Main Street	T238
Main Street	T884

Joint index table for items/sales

Item	Sales Key
Sony-TV	T57
Sony-TV	T459

Join index table linking locations and item to sales

Location	Item	Sales Key
.....	.....	.....
Main Street	Sony -TV	T57
.....	....	....

Fig. 3.7 : Join Index Tables Based on the Linkages between the Sales Fact Table and the Location and Item Dimension Tables

Example 2: Fig. 3.8 gives an example of a join index summarizing the equi-join of the relations CUSTOMER and CP on attribute cname.

Customer

CSur	CName	City	Age	Job
1	Smith	Boston	21	Clerk
2	Collins	Austin	26	Secretary
3	Ross	Austin	36	Manager
4	Jones	Paris	29	Engineer

JI

CSur	CPsur
1	2
1	3
3	1

CP

CPsur	CName	PName	City	Date
2	Smith	Jeans	2	052585
3	Smith	Shirt	4	052585
1	Ross	Jacket	3	072386

Fig. 3.8 : Join Index for Relations CUSTOMER and CP on Attribute CName

3.6.3 Efficient Processing of OLAP Queries

- As we have studied cube materialization and OLAP indexing in previous sections, the purpose of these two is to speed-up query processing in data cubes.
- Given materialized views, query processing should proceed as follows:

1. Determine which operations should be performed on the available cuboids:

- This involves transforming any selection, projection, roll-up (group-by), and drill-down operations specified in the query into corresponding SQL and/or OLAP operations.
- For example, slicing and dicing a data cube may correspond to selection and/or projection operations on a materialized cuboid.

2. Determine to which materialized cuboid(s) the relevant operations should be applied:

- This involves identifying all of the materialized cuboids that may potentially be used to answer the query, pruning(removing) the set using knowledge of "dominance" relationships among the cuboids, estimating the costs of using the remaining materialized cuboids, and selecting the cuboid with the least cost.
- Following example illustrate this process of selection of cuboid with least cost. Consider Cube "Sales" which is represented as follows:

  `"sales cube [time, item, location]: SUM(sales in dollars)"`
- The dimension hierarchies used are
  1. For Time "day < month < quarter < year"
  2. For Item "item name < brand < type"
  3. For Location "street < city < state < country"
- Also, suppose that there are four materialized cuboids available, as follows:

  cuboid 1: {year, item name, city}

  cuboid 2: {year, brand, country}

  cuboid 3: {year, brand, state}

  cuboid 4: {item name, state}, where year = 2018
- Suppose that the query to be processed is on {brand, state}, with the selection constant "year = 2018." Now we have to find that out of these four cuboids which cuboids should be selected to process the query?
- In data warehouse, Granularity means the level of detail of the data within any data structure. Finer-granularity data cannot be generated from coarser-granularity data. Therefore, cuboid 2 cannot be used because country is a more general concept than state.
- Cuboids 1, 3, and 4 can be used to process the query because:
  1. They have the same set or a superset of the dimensions in the query,
  2. The selection clause in the query can imply the selection in the cuboid, and
  3. The abstraction levels for the item and location dimensions in these cuboids are at a finer level than brand and state, respectively.
- As we can select cuboid 1, 3 and 4 but the costs of each cuboid to process the query will differ. Therefore, some cost-based estimation is required to decide which set of cuboids should be selected for query processing.
  1. The cost of cuboid 1 will be more because both item name and city are at a lower level than the brand and state concepts specified in the query.
  2. The cost of cuboid 3 will be smaller than cuboid 4, if there are not many year values associated with items in the cube, but there are several item names for each brand,
  3. Cuboid 4 could also be a better choice ,if efficient indices are available for cuboid 4.

3.7 OLAP SERVER ARCHITECTURE

- OLAP servers represents the type of OLAP systems available that can be used according to the requirement. This requirement may include the use of relational data, Multidimensional data, web based data etc.
- Specific OLAP servers are used as per the data. These servers can be classified as either Major OLAP server or Minor OLAP server.
- Major OnLine Analytical Processing (OLAP) Servers are ROLAP, HOLAP and MOLAP and are explained below.

3.7.1 MOLAP Model

- In the MOLAP model, data for analysis is stored in specialized multidimensional databases. Large multidimensional arrays form the storage structures.
- The array values indicate the location of the cells. These cells are intersections of the values of dimension attributes.
- Fig. 3.9 shows the architecture for the MOLAP model which consist of three layers in the multitier architecture.
- Precalculated and prefabricated multidimensional data cubes are stored in Multidimensional databases, (MDDB).
- The MOLAP engine in the application layer pushes a multidimensional view of the data from the MDDBs to the users. Multidimensional Database Management Systems (MDBMS) are proprietary software systems.
- The MDBMS provide the capability to consolidate and fabricate summarized cubes during the process that loads data into the MDDBS from the main data warehouse. The users who need summarized data enjoy fast response times from the pre-consolidated data.

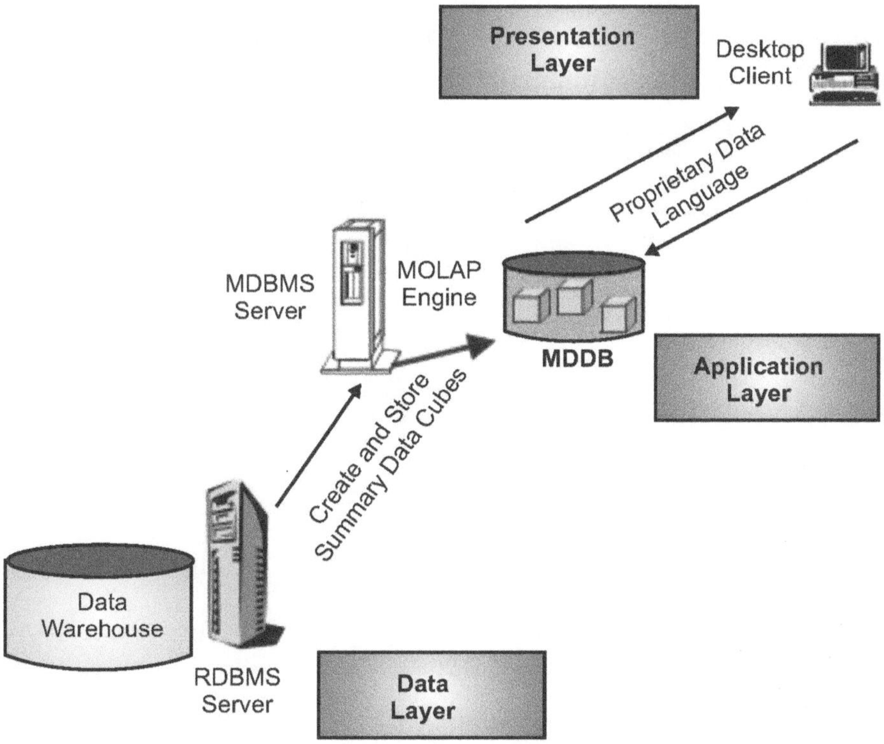

Fig. 3.9: MOLAP Model

- **For example:** Oracle Essbase and Micro strategy are the commonly used MOLAP Servers.

Advantages of MOLAP Model:

1. **Excellent Performance:** MOLAP cubes are built for fast data retrieval and are optimal for slicing and dicing operations.
2. **Can Perform Complex Calculations:** All calculations have been pre-generated when the cube is created. Hence, complex calculations are possible in quick time.

Disadvantages of MOLAP Model:

1. **Limited in the Amount of Data it can Handle:** Because all calculations are performed when the cube is built, it is not possible to include a large amount of data in the cube itself.

2. **Requires Additional Investment:** Cube technology are often proprietary and do not already exist in the organization. Therefore, to adopt MOLAP technology, chances are additional investments in human and capital resources are needed.

3.7.2 ROLAP Model

- In the ROLAP model, data is stored as rows and columns in relational form. This model presents data to the users in the form of business dimensions.
- In order to hide the storage structure to the user and present data multi-dimensionally, a semantic layer of metadata is created.
- The metadata layer supports the mapping of dimensions to the relational tables. Additional metadata supports summarizations and aggregations. You may store the metadata in relational databases.
- Fig. 3.10 shows the architecture of the ROLAP model. The analytical server in the middle tier application layer creates multidimensional views on the fly.
- The multidimensional system at the presentation layer provides a multidimensional view of the data to the users. When the users issue complex queries based on this multidimensional view, the queries are transformed into complex SQL directed to the relational database.
- Unlike the MOLAP model, static multidimensional structures are not created and stored.

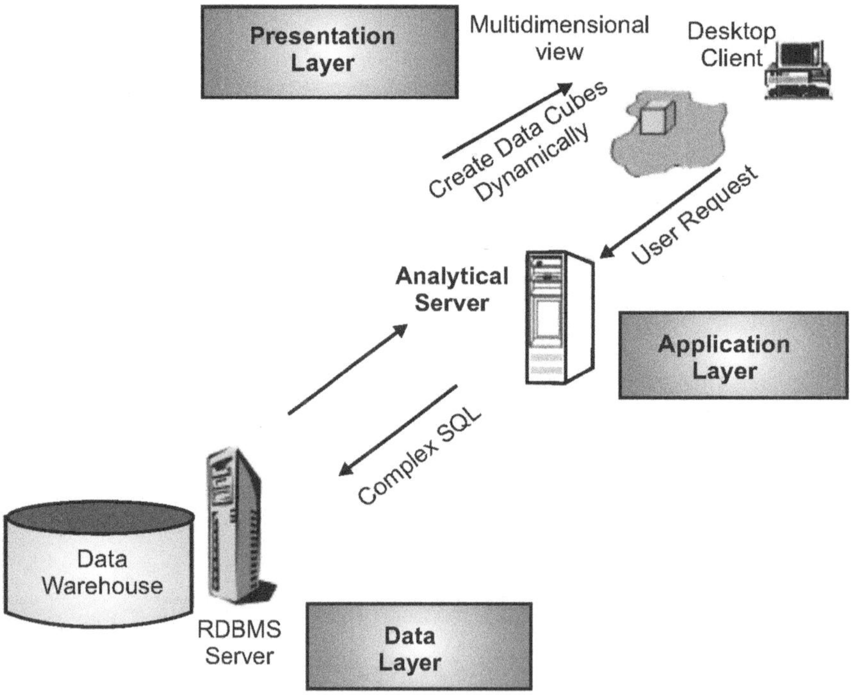

Fig. 3.10: ROLAP Model

- Local hypercubing is a variation of ROLAP provided by vendors. Following points describes how it works:
  1. The user issues a query.
  2. The results of the query get stored in a small, local, multidimensional database.
  3. The user performs analysis against this local database.
  4. If additional data is required to continue the analysis, the user issues another query and the analysis continues.
- **For example**: Oracle OLAP, Microsoft Analysis Services are the most commonly used ROLAP Servers.

Advantages of ROLAP Model:

1. Handle large amounts of data.
2. Leverage functionalities inherent in the relational database (ROLAP is based on the relational database, can therefore leverage these functionalities.)

Disadvantages of ROLAP Model:

1. **Performance:** Because each ROLAP report is essentially a SQL query and query time can be long if the underlying data size is large.
2. **Limited by SQL Functionalities:** Because ROLAP technology mainly relies on generating SQL statements to query the relational database, and SQL statements do not fit all needs (for example, it is difficult to perform complex calculations using SQL).

3.7.3 HOLAP Model

- HOLAP stands for Hybrid Online Analytical Processing System.
- HOLAP contains the best features of ROLAP and MOLAP all together making it the most efficient among all the available servers.
- HOLAP is capable of dealing with both relational databases as well as Data cube structured data sources(Multidimensional data sources). This results in flexibility and provide much larger data scalability than ROLAP and MOLAP.
- **For example :** Microsoft SQL Server is the most commonly used HOLAP Server.

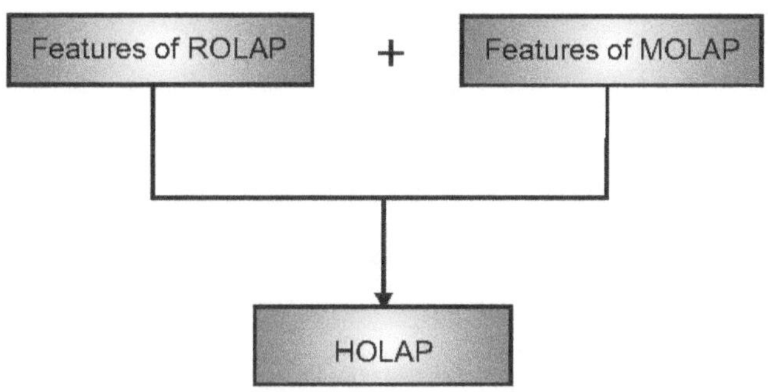

Fig. 3.11 : HOLAP

Minor Online Analytical Processing Servers :

- Minor OLAP servers also includes three of them. These are Mobile OLAP, Web OLAP and Desktop OLAP and are explained below:

1. Web OLAP:

- Web OLAP(WOLAP) system enable users to use OLAP system directly, with combination of a web browser and an internet connection.
- It makes this system more user accessible because of its client-server architecture. Also, setting up Web OLAP is very easy as only a web browser and an internet connection are needed.

2. Mobile OLAP:

- Mobile OLAP system enable users to use OLAP system directly through mobile.
- With the help of remote access feature, Mobile OLAP can be used as only a mobile device along with an internet connection are required.

3. Desktop OLAP:

- Desktop OLAP (DOLAP) uses the concept of data fragmentation. It means, a part of data from Data sources (Such as Data bases/Data Warehouses) is extracted in the form of small fragments separately on the user's desktop and knowledge discovery is done on that particular data fragment only.

- DOLAP setup requires an internet enabled Desktop/Laptop computer.

Advantages of OLAP Servers:

1. Decision Making.
2. Knowledge Discovery.
3. Data Mining.
4. Large amount of data can be processed through a single query known as decision support query.
5. OLAP servers provide consistent data outputs in the form of information, knowledge and calculations.

Disadvantages of OLAP Servers:

1. Complex structure of decision support queries.
2. Performing operations on such large data sources can lead to system hanging or freezing.
3. Prone to risk which might result into failures.
4. Slow
5. Depends totally on single field i.e. Information Technology.

Applications of OLAP Servers:

1. Report and Analytics Generation.
2. Banking.
3. Forecasting
4. Finance Sector.
5. Data Centres.

Practice Questions

1. What is data warehouse design?
2. Write steps of data warehouse design.
3. Give benefits of data warehouse usage.
4. Explain business analysis framework for data warehouse design.
5. Explain data warehouse design process.
6. How data warehouse is used for information Processing?
7. Explain the process of online analytical processing to multidimensional data mining.
8. Explain how computation is carried out in data cube.
9. What is curse of dimensionality?
10. Explain bitmap indexing with example.
11. Explain join indexing with example.
12. Explain OLAP server architecture.

✤ ✤ ✤

4...

Introduction to Data Mining

Chapter Outcomes...

- Explain concept of data mining.
- Describe the given data mining steps.
- Explain major issues for the given data.
- Explain the given data objects and attributes types.
- Describe methods of data preprocessing for the given data.
- Explain data cleaning process for the given data.

Learning Objectives...

- To understand Basic Concepts in Data Mining
- To learn Process of KDD
- To study kinds of Data can be Mined
- To understand Preprocessing and Cleaning in Data Mining

4.0 INTRODUCTION

- Today's information age a huge amount of data available and it increasing day by day. This data is of no use until it is converted into useful information. It is necessary to analyze this huge amount of data and extract useful information from it.
- Data mining is a technique that extracting information from huge sets of data. Data mining is the procedure of mining knowledge from data.
- Data mining is the process of extracting previously unknown, valid and actionable information from large data such as transaction data or database or data warehouse.
- Data mining is the process as extracting information from huge sets of data. In other words, we can say that data mining is the procedure of mining knowledge from data.
- The growth of data in various complex forms (e.g., semi-structured and unstructured, spatial and temporal, hypertext and multimedia) has been explosive owing to the rapid progress of data collection and advanced database system technologies, and the World Wide Web (WWW or Web). Therefore, an increasingly important task in data mining is to mine complex types of data.
- Data mining has emerged as a new discipline in a world of increasingly massive datasets. A dataset is a set of measurements taken from some environment or process.
- Data mining also popularly known as Knowledge Discovery in Databases (KDD), refers to the non-trivial extraction of implicit, previously unknown and potentially useful information from data in databases.

- Data mining is the process of discovering hidden, previously unknown, and usable information from a large amount of data.

Basic Terms for Data Mining:

1. **Data:**

- Data are any facts, numbers, or text that can be processed by a computer.
- Today, organizations are accumulating vast and growing amounts of data in different formats and different databases.
- This includes:
  (i) **Operational or Transactional Data,** such as sales, cost, inventory, payroll and accounting.
  (ii) **Non-Operational Data,** such as industry sales, forecast data, and macro economic data.
  (iii) **Metadata,** data about the data itself, such as logical database design or data dictionary definitions.

2. **Information:**

- The patterns, associations or relationships among all this data can provide information.
- For example, analysis of retail point of sale transaction data can yield information on which products are selling and when.

3. **Knowledge:**

- Information can be converted into knowledge about historical patterns and future trends.
- For example, summary information on retail supermarket sales can be analyzed in light of promotional efforts to provide knowledge of consumer buying behavior. Thus, a manufacturer or retailer could determine which items are most susceptible to promotional efforts.

4.1 INTRODUCTION TO DATA MINING

- Data mining is the process of collecting large amounts of raw data and transforming that data into useful information.
- The term 'Data Mining' refers to the finding of relevant and useful information from databases. Data mining and knowledge discovery in the databases is a new inter-disciplinary field, merging ideas from statistics, machine learning, databases and parallel computing.
- The rapid growth in computer technology is providing a great deal of development to the databases and information industry. This is possible due to availability of a large number of affordable data collection equipments and storage media.
- Therefore, data can be stored in huge and different kinds of databases and information repositories, which help in retrieving large volume of data and enable users to perform sophisticated analysis.
- However, an in-depth and efficient analysis becomes very difficult with such huge amount of data which originate from various sources and are in different forms for handling this problem data mining tools are used.
- Data mining tools can perform various important functions. These tools can also discover valuable knowledge from raw data present in the Databases, Data warehouses, Web, etc., and then turn into useful information.
- Data mining tasks are classified on the basis of predictive and descriptive.
  1. **Prediction Data Mining** analyzes the given dataset and basis of those behavior predict new datasets.

2. **Descriptive Data Mining** aims to finding such patterns which can describe the data so that they can easily understood by the humans.

- Data Mining is the process as extracting information from huge sets of data. In other words, we can say that data mining is the procedure of mining knowledge from data.
- Data Mining deals with exploration techniques based on advanced analytical methods and tools for handling a large amount of information.
- Data Mining is a collection of techniques for efficient automated discovery of previously unknown, valid, novel, useful and understandable patterns in large databases. The patterns must be actionable so they may be used in an enterprise's/organization's decision making.
- Data Mining, also popularly known as Knowledge Discovery in Databases (KDD), refers to the non-trivial extraction of implicit, previously unknown and potentially useful information from data in databases.

Definition of Data Mining:

- "Data mining is about extraction of interesting (non-trivial, implicit, previously unknown and potentially useful) information or patterns from data in large databases." **OR**
- "Data mining refers to extracting or mining knowledge from large amounts of data." **OR**
- "Data mining is the process of discovering hidden, previously unknown and usable information from a large amount of data. This information is represented in a compact form, often referred to as a model."

Advantages of Data Mining:

1. **Predict Future Trends:**

- Most of the working nature of the data mining systems carries on all the informational factors of the elements and their structure.
- One of the common benefits that can be derived with these data mining systems is that they can be helpful while predicting future trends.

2. **Decision Making:**

- Nowadays, all the information about anything can be determined easily with the help of technology and similarly, with the help of such technology one can make a precise decision about something unknown and unexpected.
- There are some people who make use of these data mining techniques to help them with some kind of decision making.

3. **Cost Reduction:**

- As people can collect information about the marketed products online, which eventually reduces the cost of the product and their services.

4. **Market-based Analysis:**

- Data mining process is a system where in which all the information has been gathered on the basis of market information.
- Nowadays, technology plays a crucial role in everything and that casualty can be seen in these data mining systems. Therefore, all the information collected through these data mining is basically from marketing analysis.

5. **Fast and Feasible Decisions:**

- If we want to search for information from huge amount of data, it requires lots of time. It also irritates the person who is doing such.

- Not only when a person is doing such work, the possibility of making mistakes and incorrect decision increases, but also with annoyed mind no one can make accurate decisions for sure.
- By help of data mining, we can easily get information and make fast and authentic decisions. It also helps to compare information with various factors so the decisions become more reliable.

6. **Signifies Customer Habits:**

- For example, while working in the marketing industry one can understand all the matters of customer behavior and their habits. And that is possible with the help of data mining systems.
- As these data mining systems handle all the information acquiring techniques. It is helpful in keeping the track of customer habits and their behavior.

Disadvantages of Data Mining:

1. **Violates User Privacy:**

- It is a known fact that data mining collects Personal information about people using some market-based techniques and information technology.
- Data mining system violates the privacy of its user and that is why it lacks in the matters of safety and security of its users.

2. **Additional Irrelevant Information:**

- The main functions of the data mining systems creates a relevant space for beneficial information.
- But the main problem with these information collection is that there is a possibility that the collection of information process can be little overwhelming for all.

3. **Misuse of Information:**

- Information is collected through data mining intended for the ethical purposes can be misused. This information may be exploited by unethical people or businesses to take benefits of vulnerable people or discriminate against a group of people.
- Although companies have a lot of personal information about us available online, they do not have sufficient security systems in place to protect that information.

4. **Accuracy of Data:**

- Data mining technique is not a 100 percent accurate. Most of the time while collecting information about certain elements one used to seek help from their clients, but nowadays everything has changed.
- And now the process of information collection made things easy with the mining technology and their methods. One of the most possible limitations of this data mining system is that it can provide accuracy of data with its own limits.

4.1.1 Mining Steps in Process of KDD

- Data mining is the process of collecting large amounts of raw data and transforming that data into useful information.
- Data mining is the process of discovering patterns in data. The process must be automatic or (more usually) semiautomatic.
- The patterns discovered must be meaningful in that they lead to some advantage, usually an economic one. The data is invariably present in substantial quantities.
- Many people treat data mining as a synonym for another popularly used term, Knowledge Discovery from Data or KDD while others view data mining as merely an essential step in the process of knowledge discovery.

- The knowledge discovery process is shown in Fig. 4.1 as an iterative sequence of the following steps:

Sr. No.	Steps	Explanation
1.	Data Cleaning	To remove noise and inconsistent data.
2.	Data Integration	Where multiple data sources may be combined.
3.	Data Selection	Where data relevant to the analysis task are retrieved from the database.
4.	Data Transformation	Where data are transformed and consolidated into forms appropriate for mining by performing summary or aggregation operations.
5.	Data Mining	An essential process where intelligent methods are applied to extract data patterns.
6.	Pattern Evaluation	To identify the truly interesting patterns representing knowledge based on interestingness measures.
7.	Knowledge Presentation	Where visualization and knowledge representation techniques are used to present mined knowledge to users.

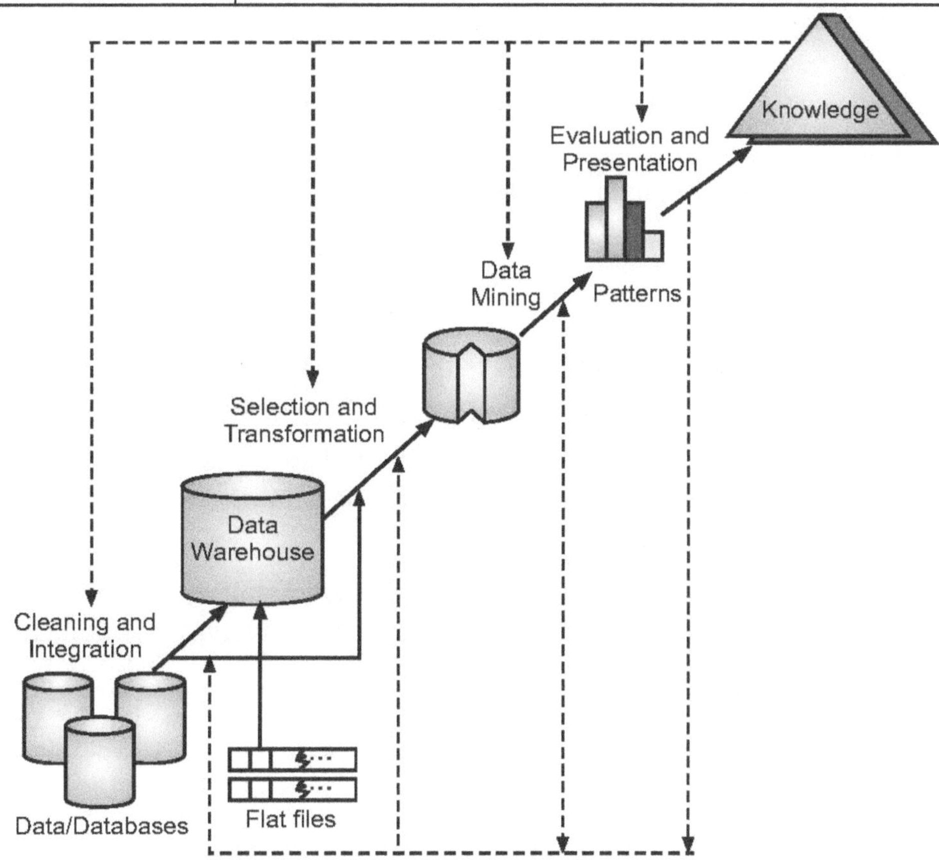

Fig. 4.1: Data Mining as a Step in the Process of Knowledge Discovery

- Steps in Fig. 4.1 are explained below:

1. **Data Cleaning:**

- Data cleaning is the process where the data gets cleaned. Data in the real world is normally incomplete, noisy and inconsistent.
- The data available in data sources might be lacking attribute values, data of interest etc. For example, we want the demographic data of customers and what if the available data does not include

attributes for the gender or age of the customers? Then the data is of course incomplete. Sometimes, the data might contain errors or outliers.

- An example, is an age attribute with value 200. It is obvious that the age value is wrong in this case. The data could also be inconsistent.
- For example, the name of an employee might be stored differently in different data tables or documents. Here, the data is inconsistent. If the data is not clean, the data mining results would be neither reliable nor accurate.
- Data cleaning involves a number of techniques including filling in the missing values manually, combined computer and human inspection, etc. The output of data cleaning process is adequately cleaned data.

2. Data Integration:

- Data integration is the process where data from different data sources are integrated into one. Data lies in different formats in different locations. Data could be stored in databases, text files, spreadsheets, documents, data cubes, Internet and so on.
- Data integration is a really complex and tricky task because data from different sources does not match normally. Suppose a table A contains an entity named customer_id where as another table B contains an entity named number.
- It is really difficult to ensure that whether both these entities refer to the same value or not. Metadata can be used effectively to reduce errors in the data integration process.
- Another issue faced is data redundancy. The same data might be available in different tables in the same database or even in different data sources.
- Data integration tries to reduce redundancy to the maximum possible level without affecting the reliability of data.

3. Data Selection:

- Data mining process requires large volumes of historical data for analysis. So, usually the data repository with integrated data contains much more data than actually required.
- From the available data, data of interest needs to be selected and stored. Data selection is the process where the data relevant to the analysis is retrieved from the database.

4. Data Transformation:

- Data transformation is the process of transforming and consolidating the data into different forms that are suitable for mining. Data transformation normally involves normalization, aggregation, generalization etc.
- For example, a data set available as "-5, 37, 100, 89, 78" can be transformed as "-0.05, 0.37, 1.00, 0.89, 0.78". Here, data becomes more suitable for data mining. After data integration, the available data is ready for data mining.

5. Data Mining:

- Data mining is the core process where a number of complex and intelligent methods are applied to extract patterns from data.
- Data mining process includes a number of tasks such as association, classification, prediction, clustering, time series analysis and so on.

6. Pattern Evaluation:

- The pattern evaluation identifies the truly interesting patterns representing knowledge based on different types of interestingness measures.

- A pattern is considered to be interesting if it is potentially useful, easily understandable by humans, validates some hypothesis that someone wants to confirm or valid on new data with some degree of certainty.

7. **Knowledge Representation:**

- The information mined from the data needs to be presented to the user in an appealing way. Different knowledge representation and visualization techniques are applied to provide the output of data mining to the users.
- Steps 1 through 4 are different forms of data preprocessing, where data are prepared for mining. The data mining step may interact with the user or a knowledge base. The interesting patterns are presented to the user and may be stored as new knowledge in the knowledge base.
- The preceding view shows data mining as one step in the knowledge discovery process, albeit an essential one because it uncovers hidden patterns for evaluation.
- However, in industry, in media, and in the research, the term Data Mining is often used to refer to the entire knowledge discovery process. Therefore, we adopt a broad view of data mining functionality.
- Data Mining is the process of discovering interesting patterns and knowledge from large amounts of data. The data sources can include databases, data warehouses, the Web, other information repositories, or data that are streamed into the system dynamically.

4.1.2 Data Mining Tasks

- A data mining task can be specified in the form of a data mining query, which is input to the data mining system.
- The said functionalities are measured to perceive the type of patterns to be found in data mining tasks. Data mining tasks can be categorized in to following two categories:
    1. **Descriptive Task:** These tasks present the general properties of data stored in database. The descriptive tasks are used to find out patterns in data i.e. cluster, correlation, trends and anomalies etc.
    2. **Predictive Tasks:** Predictive data mining tasks predict the value of one attribute on the bases of values of other attributes, which is known as target or dependent variable and the attributes used for making the prediction are known as independent variables.

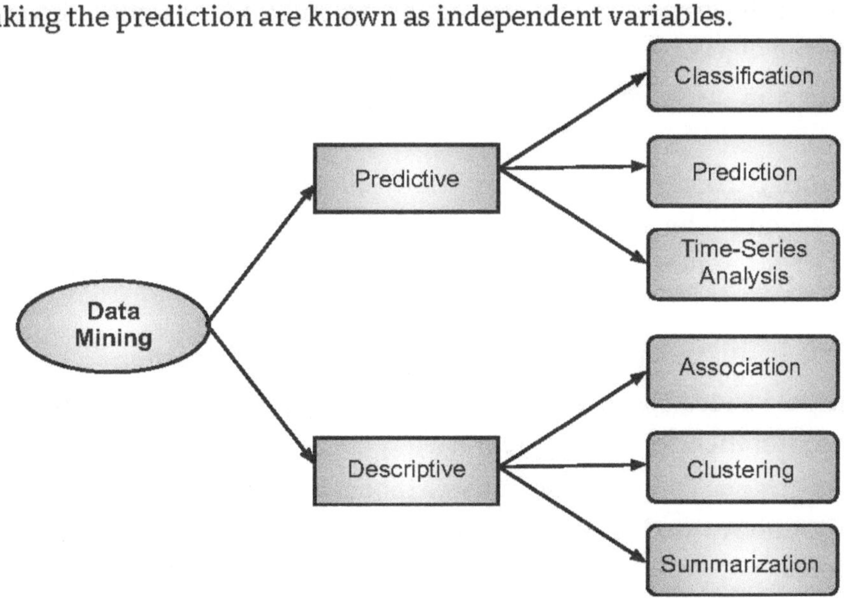

Fig. 4.2 : Tasks in Data Mining

- Tasks of data mining in Fig. 4.2 are explained below:

1. **Classification:**

- Classification derives a model to determine the class of an object based on its attributes. A collection of records will be available, each record with a set of attributes.
- One of the attributes will be class attribute and the goal of classification task is assigning a class attribute to new set of records as accurately as possible.
- Classification can be used in direct marketing, that is to reduce marketing costs by targeting a set of customers who are likely to buy a new product. Using the available data, it is possible to know which customers purchased similar products and who did not purchase in the past.
- Hence, (purchase, don't purchase) decision forms the class attribute in this case. Once the class attribute is assigned, demographic and lifestyle information of customers who purchased similar products can be collected and promotion mails can be sent to them directly.

2. **Prediction:**

- Prediction task predicts the possible values of missing or future data.
- Prediction involves developing a model based on the available data and this model is used in predicting future values of a new data set of interest.
- For example, a model can predict the income of an employee based on education, experience and other demographic factors like place of stay, gender etc. Also prediction analysis is used in different areas including medical diagnosis, fraud detection etc.

3. **Time - Series Analysis**:

- Time series is a sequence of events where the next event is determined by one or more of the preceding events.
- Time series reflects the process being measured and there are certain components that affect the behavior of a process.
- Time series analysis includes methods to analyze time-series data in order to extract useful patterns, trends, rules and statistics. Stock market prediction is an important application of time- series analysis.

4. **Association:**

- Association discovers the association or connection among a set of items. Association identifies the relationships between objects.
- Association analysis is used for commodity management, advertising, catalog design, direct marketing etc.
- A retailer can identify the products that normally customers purchase together or even find the customers who respond to the promotion of same kind of products. If a retailer finds that bread and butter are bought together mostly, he can put butter on sale to promote the sale of bread.

5. **Clustering:**

- Clustering is used to identify data objects that are similar to one another.
- The similarity can be decided based on a number of factors like purchase behavior, responsiveness to certain actions, geographical locations and so on.
- For example, an insurance company can cluster its customers based on age, residence, income etc. This group information will be helpful to understand the customers better and hence provide better customized services.

6. **Summarization:**

- Summarization is the generalization of data. A set of relevant data is summarized which result in a smaller set that gives aggregated information of the data.
- For example, the shopping done by a customer can be summarized into total products, total spending, offers used, etc. Such high level summarized information can be useful for sales or customer relationship team for detailed customer and purchase behavior analysis.
- Data can be summarized in different abstraction levels and from different angles.

4.2 WHAT TYPE OF DATA CAN BE MINED?

- The most basic forms of data for mining applications are database data, data warehouse data and transactional data as explained below:

1. **Database Data:**

- A database system, also called a database management system (DBMS), consists of a collection of interrelated data, known as a database, and a set of software programs to manage and access the data.
- A relational database is a collection of tables, each of which is assigned a unique name. Each table consists of a set of attributes (columns or fields) and usually stores a large set of tuples (records or rows). Each tuple in a relational table represents an object identified by a unique key and described by a set of attribute values.
- Relational data can be accessed by database queries written in a relational query language (e.g., SQL) or with the assistance of graphical user interfaces.

2. **Data Warehouse:**

- A data warehouse is a repository of information collected from multiple sources, stored under a unified schema, and usually residing at a single site.
- Data warehouses are constructed via a process of data cleaning, data integration, data transformation, data loading, and periodic data refreshing.
- A data warehouse is a large data repository that aggregates data usually from multiple sources or segments of a business, without the data being necessarily related.
- A data warehouse is usually modeled by a multidimensional data structure, called a data cube, in which each dimension corresponds to an attribute or a set of attributes in the schema, and each cell stores the value of some aggregate measure such as count or sum, sales_ amount.
- A data cube provides a multidimensional view of data and allows the precomputation and fast access of summarized data.
- A data lake is a large data repository that stores unstructured data that is classified and tagged with metadata.
- Data marts are subsets of the data repository. These data marts are more targeted to what the data user needs and easier to use.
- Data marts also are more secure because they limit authorized users to isolated data sets. Those users cannot access all the data in the data repository.
- Metadata repositories store data about data and databases. The metadata explains where the data source, how it was captured and what it represents.

3. **Transactional Data:**

- Each record in a transactional database captures a transaction, such as a customer's purchase, a flight booking, or a user's clicks on a web page.

- A transaction typically includes a unique transaction identity number (trans ID) and a list of the items making up the transaction, such as the items purchased in the transaction.
- Fig. 4.3 shows a sample transactional database.

Trans_ID	List_of_item_IDs
T100	I1, I2, I8, I16
T200	I2, I8
...	...

Fig. 4.3

- Data mining can also be applied to other forms of data as shown in following table.(e.g., data streams, ordered/sequence data, graph or networked data, spatial data, text data, multimedia data, and the WWW).

Sr. No.	Types of Data	Meaning	Source
1.	Time-related or Sequence data	Sequential data is any kind of data where the order matters A time series is a sequence taken at successive equally spaced points in time and it is not the only case of sequential data.	Historical records, stock exchange data, and time-series and biological sequence data.
2.	Data Streams	Stream data flow in and out of a computer system continuously and with varying update rates. Uninterrupted flow of a long sequence of data, such as in audio and video data files.	Video surveillance and sensor data, which are continuously transmitted),
3.	Text Data	Text databases consist of huge collection of documents	Text document.
4.	Spatial Data	spatial data represents the location, size and shape of an object on planet Earth such as a building, lake, mountain or township.	Maps.
5.	Hypertext and Multimedia Data	Hypertext is the grouping of relevant information in the form of nodes which are connected through some links. Multimedia is the combining of different media types for example sound, animation, text, graphics and video	Including text, image, video, and audio data.
6.	Graph and Networked Data	A graph is a non linear data structure consisting of nodes and edges.	Social and information networks
7.	Web Data	Data obtained from WWW or Web.	A huge, widely distributed information repository made available by the Internet

4.2.1 Issues in Data Mining

- Data mining systems face a lot of challenges and issues in today's world. Some of them are mining methodology and user interaction issues, performance issues, issues relating to the diversity of database types etc.

1. **Mining Methodology and User Interaction Issues:**
   (i) **Mining different Kinds of Knowledge in Databases**: Different user - different knowledge - different way. That means different client want a different kind of information so it becomes difficult to cover vast range of data that can meet the client requirement.
   (ii) **Interactive Mining of Knowledge at Multiple Levels of Abstraction:** Interactive mining allows users to focus the search for patterns from different angles. The data mining process should be interactive because it is difficult to know what can be discovered within a database.
   (iii) **Incorporation of Background Knowledge:** Background knowledge is used to guide discovery process and to express the discovered patterns.
   (iv) **Query Languages and Ad-hoc Mining:** Relational query languages (such as SQL) allow users to pose ad-hoc queries for data retrieval. The language of data mining query language should be in perfectly matched with the query language of data warehouse.
   (v) **Handling Noisy or Incomplete Data:** In a large database, many of the attribute values will be incorrect. This may be due to human error or because of any instruments fail. Data cleaning methods and data analysis methods are used to handle noise data.
2. **Performance Issues:**
   (i) **Efficiency and Scalability of Data Mining Algorithms:** To effectively extract information from a huge amount of data in databases, data mining algorithms must be efficient and scalable.
   (ii) **Parallel, Distributed and Incremental Mining Algorithms:** The huge size of many databases, the wide distribution of data, and complexity of some data mining methods are factors motivating the development of parallel and distributed data mining algorithms. Such algorithms divide the data into partitions, which are processed in parallel.
3. **Issues Related to the Diversity of Database Types:**
   (i) **Handling of Relational and Complex Types of Data:** There are many kinds of data stored in databases and data warehouses. It is not possible for one system to mine all these kind of data.So different data mining system should be construed for different kinds data.
   (ii) **Mining Information from Heterogeneous Databases and Global Information Systems:** Since data is fetched from different data sources on Local Area Network (LAN) and Wide Area Network (WAN). The discovery of knowledge from different sources of structured is a great challenge to data mining.
4. **Accuracy of Data Issues:**
   - Data mining technique is not a 100 percent accurate. Most of the time while collecting information about certain elements one used to seek help from their clients, but nowadays everything has changed.
   - And now the process of information collection made things easy with the mining technology and their methods. One of the most possible limitations of this data mining system is that it can provide accuracy of data with its own limits.

4.3 DATA OBJECTS AND ATTRIBUTES

- Data objects are the essential part of a database. A data object represents the entity.
- Data Objects are like group of attribute of an entity. For example, a sales data object may represent customer, sales or purchases. Data objects are typically described by attributes.
- Data objects are also referred as samples, examples, instances, data points, or objects. If the data objects a restored in a database, they are data tuples. Here the rows of a database correspond to the data objects, and the columns correspond to the attributes.
- An attribute is a data field, representing a characteristic or feature of a data object. Attributes are also referred as dimension, feature, and variable.
- Data warehousing uses term dimension to represent an attribute whereas Machine learning uses the term feature, and statisticians prefer the term variable.
- Data is information typically the results of measurement (numerical) or counting (categorical). Attributes/Variables serve as placeholders for data. There are two types of attributes/variables, numerical and categorical.

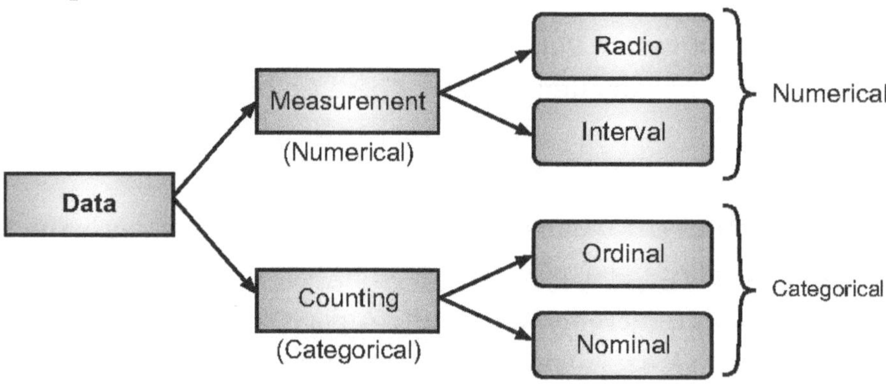

Fig. 4.4

1. **Numerical Attributes/Continuous Attributes:**

- A numerical or continuous variable (attribute) is one that may take on any value within a finite or infinite interval (e.g., height, weight, temperature, blood glucose). There are two types of numerical attributes namely, interval and ratio.
- Interval attributes are measured on a scale of equal-size units. The values of interval attributes have order and can be positive, 0, or negative. Thus, in addition to providing a ranking of values, such attributes allow us to compare and quantify the difference between values. A good example is temperature in Centigrade degrees.
- Data on an interval scale can be added and subtracted but cannot be meaningfully multiplied or divided. For example, we cannot say that one day is twice as hot as another day.
- In contrast, a ratio attribute has values with a true zero and can be added, subtracted, multiplied or divided.
- A ratio attribute values are ordered, and we can also compute the difference between values, as well as the mean, median, and mode. Example of Ratio attributes are weight, height, latitude and longitude.

- Following are the statistics and visualization method applicable on numerical data.

Sr. No.	Statistics	Visualization	Equation	Description
1.	Count	Histogram	N	The number of values (observations) of the variable.
2.	Minimum	Box Plot	Min	The smallest value of the variable.
3.	Maximum	Box Plot	Max	The largest value of the variable.
4.	Mean	Box Plot	$\bar{X} = \frac{\Sigma X}{N}$	The sum of the values divided by the count.
5.	Median	Box Plot	$\tilde{X}$	The middle value. Below and above median lies an equal number of values.
6.	Mode	Histogram	-	The most frequent value. There can be more than one mode.
7.	Quantile	Box Plot	Q_X	A set of 'cut points' that divide a set of data into groups containing equal numbers of values (Quartile, Quintile, Percentile).
8.	Range	Box Plot	Max-Min	The difference between maximum and minimum.
9.	Variance	Histogram	$S^2 = \frac{\Sigma(X-\bar{X})^2}{N-1}$	A measure of data dispersion.
10.	Standard Deviation	Histogram	$S = \sqrt{S^2}$	The square root of variance.
11.	Coefficient of Deviation	Histogram	$CV = \frac{S}{\bar{X}} \times 100\ \%$	A measure of data dispersion divided by mean.
12.	Skewness	Histogram	$\frac{N}{(N-1)(N-2)} \sum \left(\frac{X-\bar{X}}{S}\right)^3$	A measure of symmetry or asymmetry in the distribution of data.
13.	Kurtosis	Histogram	$\left[\frac{N(N+1)}{(N-1)(N-2)(N-3)} \sum \left(\frac{X-\bar{X}}{S}\right)^4\right] - \frac{3(N-1)^2}{(N-2)(N-3)}$	A measure of whether the data are peaked or flat relative to a normal distribution.

2. Categorical Attributes/Discrete Attributes:

- A categorical or discrete attribute is one that has two or more categories (values). There are three types of categorical attributes, nominal, binary and ordinal.
- The nominal, binary, and ordinal attributes are qualitative. That is, they describe a feature of an object without giving an actual size or quantity. The values of such qualitative attributes are typically words representing categories.

(i) Nominal Attributes:

- Nominal means "relating to names." The values of a nominal attribute are symbols or names of things. Each value represents some kind of category, code, or state, and so nominal attributes are also referred to as categorical.
- A nominal attributes has no intrinsic ordering to its categories. For example, gender is a categorical attributes having two categories (male and female) with no intrinsic ordering to the categories.
- Because nominal attribute values do not have any meaningful order about them and are not quantitative, it makes no sense to find the mean (average) value or median (middle) value for such an attribute, given a set of objects.

(ii) Binary Attribute :

- A binary attribute is a nominal attribute with only two categories or states: 0 or 1, where 0 typically means that the attribute is absent, and 1 means that it is present. Binary attributes are referred to as Boolean if the two states correspond to true and false.
- A binary attribute is symmetric if both of its states are equally valuable and carry the same weight; that is, there is no preference on which outcome should be coded as 0 or 1. One such example could be the attribute gender having the states male and female.
- A binary attribute is asymmetric if the outcomes of the states are not equally important, such as the positive and negative outcomes of a medical test for HIV. By convention, we code the most important outcome, which is usually the rarest one, by 1 (e.g., HIV positive) and the other by 0 (e.g., HIV negative).

(iii) Ordinal Attributes :

- An ordinal attribute has a clear ordering. For example, temperature as attribute with three orderly categories (low, medium and high). The central tendency of an ordinal attribute can be represented by its mode and its median (the middle value in an ordered sequence), but the mean cannot be defined.
- A frequency table is a way of counting how often each category of the attribute in question occurs. It may be enhanced by the addition of percentages that fall into each category.
- **Example:** The housing attribute with three categories (For Free, Own and Rent).

Frequency Table

Housing	Count	Count%
For Free	96	10.67%
Own	641	71.22%
Rent	163	18.11%

Housing

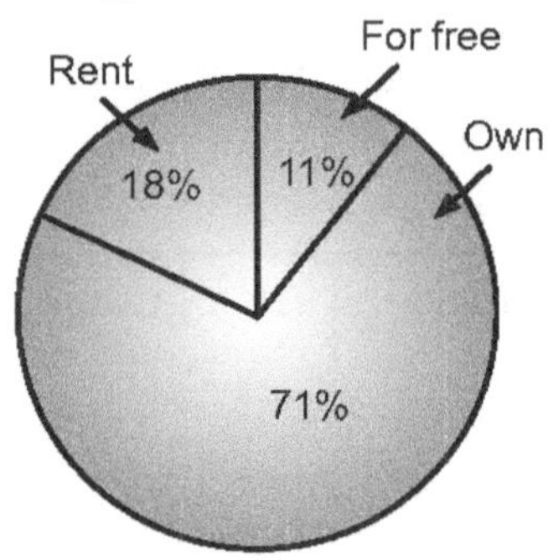

Housing

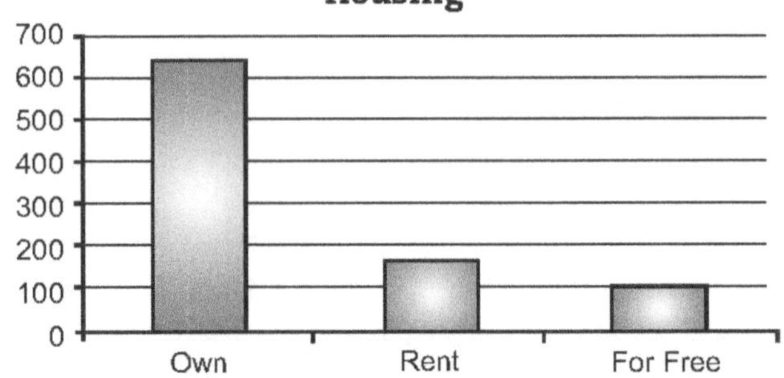

Fig. 4.5

4.4 DATA PREPROCESSING

- Raw data (real world data) is always incomplete and that data cannot be sent through a model. That would cause certain errors. That is why we need to preprocess data before sending through a model.
- Data in the real world is incomplete, noisy and inconsistent as explained below:
  1. **Incomplete:** Lacking attribute values, lacking certain attributes of interest or containing only aggregate data %.
  2. **Noisy:** Containing errors or outliers %.
  3. **Inconsistent:** Containing discrepancies in codes or names.
- Data preprocessing is a data mining technique that transforms raw data into an understandable format.

4.4.1 Why Preprocess the Data?

- Bad data quality can lead to inaccurate and slow decision-making. Improving data quality is much more than "clearing" out bad data; it's a dedicated process that involves considering all aspects of the collection process.
- Data have quality if they satisfy the requirements of the intended use. There are many factors comprising data quality, including accuracy, completeness, consistency, timeliness, believability, and interpretability.
- Fig. 4.6 shows factors for data quality:

1. **Completeness:**

- Completeness is defined as expected comprehensiveness. Data can be complete even if optional data is missing. As long as the data meets the expectations then the data is considered complete.
- For example, a customer's first name and last name are mandatory but middle name is optional; so a record can be considered complete even if a middle name is not available.

2. **Consistency:**

- Consistency means data across all systems reflects the same information and are in synch with each other across the enterprise.
- **Examples:** A business unit status is closed but there are sales for that business unit. Employee status is terminated but pay status is active.

3. **Conformity:**

- Conformity means the data is following the set of standard data definitions like data type, size and format.
- **For example,** date of birth of customer is in the format "mm/dd/yyyy".

4. **Accuracy:**

- Accuracy is the degree to which data correctly reflects the real world object OR an event being described.
- **Examples :** Sales of the business unit are the real value. Address of an employee in the employee database is the real address.

5. **Integrity:**

- Integrity means validity of data across the relationships and ensures that all data in a database can be traced and connected to other data.

- For example, in a customer database, there should be a valid customer, addresses and relationship between them. If there is an address relationship data without a customer then that data is not valid and is considered an orphaned record.

Fig. 4.6

6. **Timeliness:**

- Timeliness references whether information is available when it is expected and needed. Timeliness of data is very important.
- This is reflected in companies/organizations that are required to publish their quarterly results within a given frame of time, Customer service providing up-to date information to the customers, Credit system checking in real-time on the credit card account activity.
- The timeliness depends on user expectation. Online availability of data could be required for room allocation system in hospitality, but nightly data could be perfectly acceptable for a billing system.

7. **Believability and Interpretability:**

- Believability reflects how much the data are trusted by users, while interpretability reflects how easy the data are understood.
- Suppose that a database, at one point, had several errors, all of which have since been corrected. The past errors, however, had caused many problems for sales department users, and so they no longer trust the data.
- The data also use many accounting codes, which the sales department does not know how to interpret.
- Even though the database is now accurate, complete, consistent, and timely, sales department users may regard it as of low quality due to poor believability and interpretability.

4.4.2 Major Task in Preprocessing

- Following table shows the basic preprocessing steps require on data to send it through a model.

Sr. No.	Preprocessing Steps	Meaning
1.	Data Cleanings	Fill in missing values, smooth noisy data, identify or remove outliers, and resolve inconsistencies.
2.	Data Integration	Integration of multiple databases, data cubes or files.

Contd....

Sr. No.	Preprocessing Steps	Meaning
3.	Data Transformation	Normalization and aggregation.
4.	Data Reduction	Obtains reduced representation in volume but produces the same or similar analytical results.
5.	Data Discretization	Part of data reduction but with particular importance, especially for numerical data.

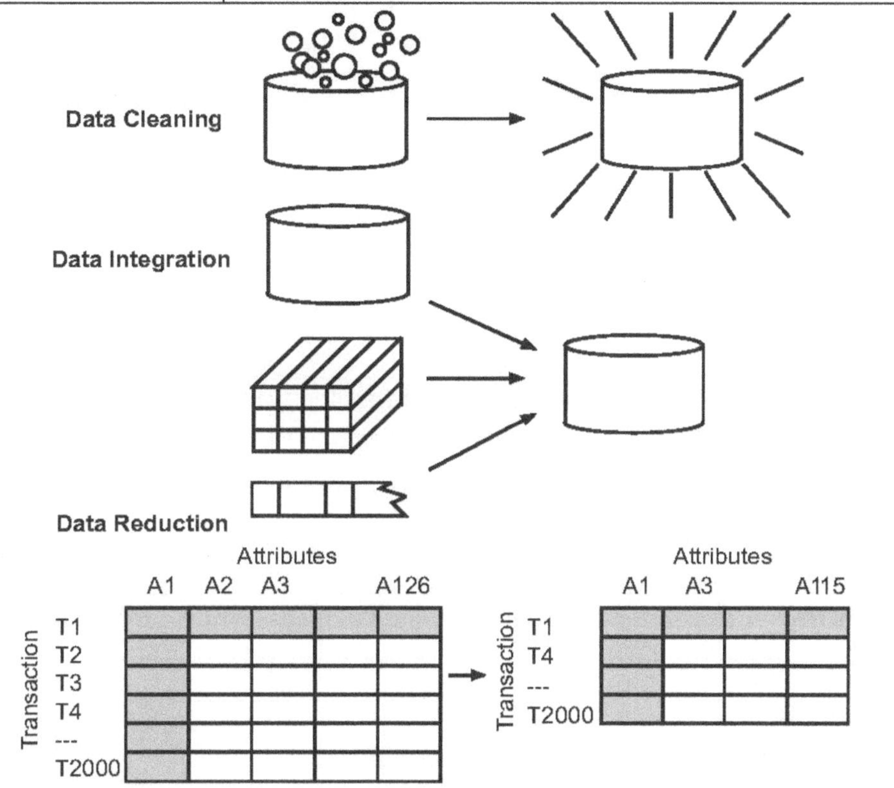

Fig. 4.7: Forms of Data Preprocessing

1. Data Cleaning:

- Real world data tend to be incomplete, noisy, and inconsistent. Data cleaning (or data cleansing) routines attempt to fill in missing values, smooth out noise while identifying outliers, and correct inconsistencies in the data.

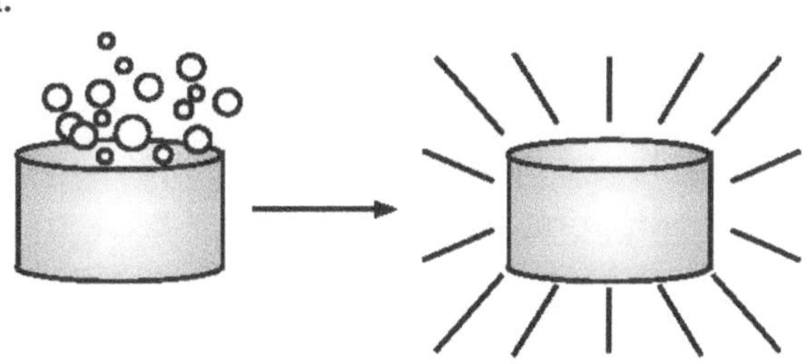

Fig. 4.8: Data Cleaning

- The detailed about data cleaning is explained in Section 4.5.

2. Data Integration:

- Data integration is one of the steps of data pre-processing that involves combining data residing in different sources and providing users with a unified view of these data.

- It merges the data from multiple data stores (data sources). It includes multiple databases, data cubes or flat files.
- There are mainly two major approaches for data integration - commonly known as "tight coupling approach" and "loose coupling approach".

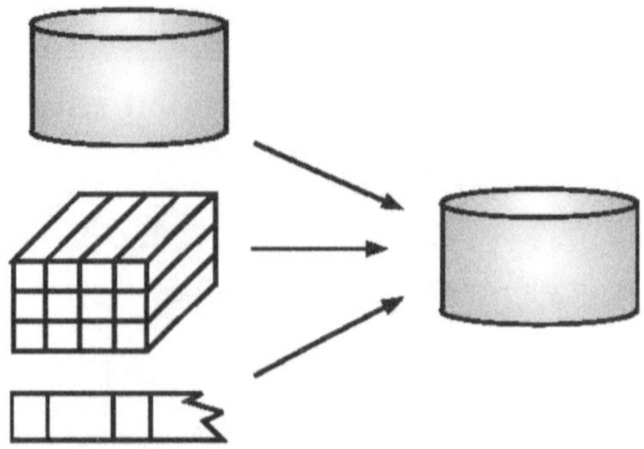

Fig. 4.9: Data Integration

(I) Tight Coupling:

- Here, data is pulled over from different sources into a single physical location through the process of ETL (Extraction, Transformation and Loading).
- The single physical location provides an uniform interface for querying the data. ETL layer helps to map the data from the sources so as to provide a uniform data warehouzse.
- This approach is called tight coupling since in this approach the data is tightly coupled with the physical repository at the time of query.

Advantages:

(i) Independence, (lesser dependency to source systems since data is physically copied over).

(ii) Faster query processing.

(iii) Complex query processing.

(iv) Advanced data summarization and storage possible.

(v) High volume data processing.

Disadvantages:

(i) Latency as data needs to be loaded using ETL.

(ii) Costlier as data localization, infrastructure, security required.

(II) Loose Coupling:

- Here, a virtual mediated schema provides an interface that takes the query from the user, transforms it in a way the source database can understand and then sends the query directly to the source databases to obtain the result.
- In this approach, the data only remains in the actual source databases. However, mediated schema contains several "adapters" or "wrappers" that can connect back to the source systems in order to bring the data to the front end.

Advantages:

(i) Data freshness because of low latency.

(ii) Higher agility i.e. when a new source system comes or existing source system changes - only the corresponding adapter is created or changed - largely not affecting the other parts of the system.

(iii) Less costlier as lot of infrastructure cost can be saved since data localization not required.

Disadvantages:

(i) Semantic conflicts.

(ii) Slower query response.

(iii) High order dependency to the data sources.

- For example, let's imagine that an electronics company is preparing to roll out a new mobile device. The marketing department might want to retrieve customer information from a sales department database and compare it to information from the product department to create a targeted sales list.
- A good data integration system would let the marketing department view information from both sources in a unified way, leaving out any information that didn't apply to the search.

2. Data Transformation:

- In data mining pre-processes and especially in metadata and data warehouse, we use data transformation in order to convert data from a source data format into destination data.

$$-2, 32, 100, 59, 48 \longrightarrow -0.02, 0.32, 1.00, 0.59, 0.48$$

Fig. 4.10: Data Transformation

- Here, the data are transformed or consolidated into forms appropriate for mining. Data transformation operations would contribute toward the success of the mining process.
- Data transformation can involve the following:

(i) Smoothing: It helps to remove noise from the data. It is a form of data cleaning where users specify transformations to correct data inconsistencies. Such techniques include binning, regression and clustering as already explained in Section 2.3.1, Point (ii).

(ii) Aggregation: here Summary or aggregation operations are applied to the data. I.e., the weekly sales data is aggregated to calculate the monthly and yearly total. This step is typically used in constructing a data cube for analysis of the data at multiple granularities. Aggregation is a form of data reduction.

(iii) Generalization: In this step, Low-level/Primitive data is replaced by higher-level concepts with the help of concept hierarchies. For example, the city is replaced by the county. For example, attributes, like age, may be mapped to higher-level concepts, like youth, middle-aged, and senior. Generalization is a form of data reduction.

(iv) Normalization: Normalization performed when the attribute data are scaled up or scaled down. Here the attribute data are scaled so as to fall within a small specified range, such as 1:0 to 1:0, or 0:0 to 1:0.Normalization is particularly useful for classification algorithms involving neural networks, or distance measurements such as nearest-neighbor classification and clustering. There are three methods for data normalization:

(a) min-max Normalization :

- Performs a linear transformation on the original data
- Suppose that min A and max A are the minimum and maximum values of an attribute, A.
- Min-max normalization maps a value, V, of A to V_0 in the range [new min A; new max A] by computing

$$V_0 = \frac{V - \text{minA}}{\text{maxA} - \text{minA}} (\text{new max A} - \text{new min A})$$

- min-max normalization preserves the relationships among the original data values.

- Suppose that the minimum and maximum values for the feature income are \$120,00 and \$98,000, respectively. We would like to map income to the range 0.0 to 1.0. By min-max normalization, a value of \$73,600 for income is transformed to:

$$\frac{73,600-12,000}{98,000-12,000}(1.0-0.0)+0.0=0.716$$

(b) z-score Normalization:

- Here, the values for an attribute, A are normalized based on the mean and standard deviation of A.
- Value, V of A is normalized to V_0 by computing

$$V_0=\frac{V-\bar{A}}{\sigma A}$$

where, $\bar{A}$ and σA are the mean and standard deviation, respectively.

- This method of normalization is useful when the actual minimum and maximum of attribute Aare unknown or when there are outliers that dominate the min-max normalization.
- Suppose that the mean and standard deviation of the values for the feature income are \$54,000 and \$16,000, respectively. With z-score normalization, a value of \$73,6000 for income is transformed to:

$$\frac{73,600-54,000}{16,000}=1.225$$

(c) Normalization by Decimal Scaling:

- Here, the normalization is done by moving the decimal point of values of attribute A.The number of decimal points moved depends on the maximum absolute value of A.
- Value, V of A is normalized to V_0 by computing
- Normalized value of attribute $V_0 = (V_i / 10_j)$
  where, j is the smallest integer such that Max $(|V_0|) < 1$.
- Suppose that the recorded values of F range from −986 to 917. The maximum absolute value of is 986. To normalize by decimal scaling, we therefore divide each value by 1,000 (i.e., j = 3) so that −986 normalizes to −0.986 and 917 normalizes to 0.917.

(v) Attribute Construction: Here, new attributes are constructed and added from the given set of attributes to help the mining process. Attribute construction helps to improve the accuracy and understanding of structure in high-dimensional data. By combining attributes, attribute construction can discover missing information about the relationships between data attributes that can be useful for knowledge discovery.

Example: The structure of stored data may vary between applications, requiring semantic mapping prior to the transformation process. For instance, two applications might store the same customer credit card information using slightly different structures:

Application A	Example	Application B	Example
Cardholder First Name	JOHN	Cardholder Name	JOHNDOE
Cardholder Last Name	DOE	Card Type	VISA
Card Type and Card Number	VISA 0 1 2 3 4 5 6 7 8 9 10 11 12	Card Number	0123 4567 8910 11 12
Expiration Date	05/2012	Expiration Date	05/2012

- To ensure that critical data isn't lost when the two applications are integrated, information from Application A needs to be reorganized to fit the data structure of Application B.

4. Data Reduction:

- A database or date warehouse may store terabytes of data.So it may take very long to perform data analysis and mining on such huge amounts of data.
- Data reduction techniques can be applied to obtain a reduced representation of the data set that is much smaller in volume, yet closely maintains the integrity of the original data.
- That is, mining on the reduced data set should be more efficient yet produce the same (or almost the same) analytical results.
- Following are approaches through which we achieve data reduction:

(i) Data Cube Aggregation:

- It reduces the data to the concept level needed in the analysis. Queries regarding aggregated information should be answered using data cube when possible.
- Data cubes store multidimensional aggregated information.
- Fig. 4.11 shows a data cube for multidimensional analysis of sales data with respect to annual sales per item type for each branch.
- Each cells holds an aggregate data value, corresponding to the data point in multidimensional space.
- Data cubes provide fast access to precomputed, summarized data, thereby benefiting on-line analytical processing as well as data mining.

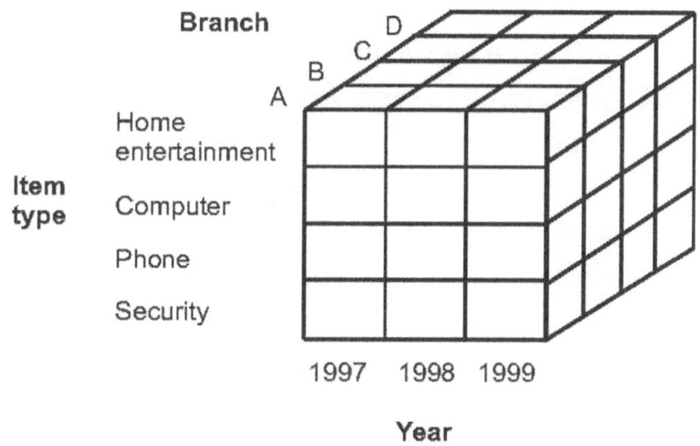

Fig. 4.11

- Data cubes created for varying levels of abstraction are sometimes referred to as cuboids, so that a "data cube" may instead refer to a lattice of cuboids. Each higher level of abstraction further reduces the resulting data size.
- The cube created at the lowest level of abstraction is referred to as the base cuboid. A cube for the highest level of abstraction is the apex cuboid.
- The following database consists of sales per quarter for the years 1997-1999.

Year = 1999

Year = 1998

Year = 1997	
Quarter	Sales
Q1	$224,000
Q2	$408,000
Q3	$350,000
Q4	$586,000

→

Year	Sales
1997	$1,568,000
1998	$2,356,000
1999	$3,594,000

Fig. 4.12

- Suppose, the analyzer interested in the annual sales rather than sales per quarter, the above data can be aggregated so that the resulting data summarizes the total sales per year instead of per quarter.
- The resulting data in smaller in volume, without loss of information necessary for the analysis task.

(ii) Attribute Subset Selection:

- The purpose of attribute subset selection is to detect and remove irrelevant weakly relevant or redundant characteristics or dimensions present in data.
- Basic heuristic methods of attribute subset selection include the following techniques, some of which are illustrated below:

(a) **Step-Wise Forward Selection:** The procedure starts with an empty set of attributes. The best of the original attributes is determined and added to the set. At each subsequent iteration or step, the best of the remaining original attributes is added to the set.

(b) **Step-Wise Backward Elimination:** The procedure starts with the full set of attributes. At each step, it removes the worst attribute remaining in the set.

(c) **Combination Forward Selection and Backward Elimination:** The step-wise forward selection and backward elimination methods can be combined, where at each step one selects the best attribute and removes the worst from among the remaining attributes.

(d) **Decision Tree Induction:** Decision tree induction constructs a flow-chart-like structure where each internal (non-leaf) node denotes a test on an attribute, each branch corresponds to an outcome of the test, and each external (leaf) node denotes a class prediction. At each node, the algorithm chooses the "best" attribute to partition the data into individual classes. When decision tree induction is used for attribute subset selection, a tree is constructed from the given data. All attributes that do not appear in the tree are assumed to be irrelevant. The set of attributes appearing in the tree form the reduced subset of attributes.

Forward Selection	Backward Elimination	Decision Tree Induction
Initial Attribute Set: {A1, A2, A3, A4, A5, A6} **Initial Reduced Set:** {} -> {A1} --> {A1, A4} --->**Reduced Attribute Set:** {A1, A4, A6}	**Initial Attribute Set:** {A1, A2, A3, A4, A5, A6} -> {A1, A3, A4, A5, A6} --> {A1, A4, A5, A6} --->**Reduced Attribute Set:** {A1, A4, A6}	**Initial Attribute Set:** {A1, A2, A3, A4, A5, A6} 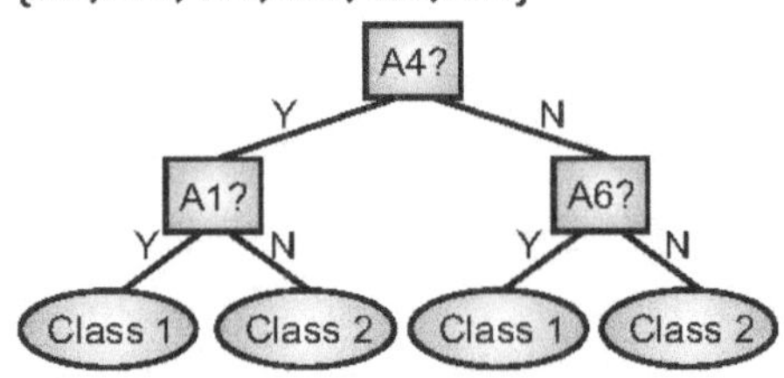 --->**Reduced Attribute Set:** {A1, A4, A6}

Fig. 4.13: Greedy (Heuristic) Methods for Attribute Subset Selection

(i) **Dimensionality Reduction:** In dimensionality reduction redundant attributes are detected and removed which reduce the data set size. Also encoding mechanisms are used to reduce the dataset size.

(ii) **Numerosity Reduction:** Data is replaced or estimated by alternative, smaller data representations such as parametric models (which stores only the model parameters instead of the actual data) or nonparametric methods such as clustering, sampling, and the use of histograms.

(iii) Data Compression: Transformations are applied to obtain a reduced or "compressed" representation of the original data. If the original data can be reconstructed from the compressed data without any information loss, the data reduction is called lossless. If, instead, we can reconstruct only an approximation of the original data, then the data reduction is **called There are several lossless algorithms** for string compression; however, they typically allow only limited data manipulation. Dimensionality reduction and numerosity reduction techniques can also be considered forms of data compression.

(iv) Sampling: Selecting a subset of the data objects to be analyzed. Sampling is commonly used approach for selecting a subset of the data to be analyzed. Typically used because it is too expensive or time consuming to process all the data.

(v) Feature Selection: Selecting a subset of the features to be analyzed. Select a minimal set of features such that the probability distribution of the class is close to the one obtained by all the features.

5. Data Discretization:

- Discretization and concept hierarchy generation are powerful tools for data mining, in that they allow the mining of data at multiple levels of abstraction.
- Data discretization and concept hierarchy generation are also forms of data reduction. The raw data are replaced by a smaller number of interval or concept labels. This simplifies the original data and makes the mining more efficient.
- The resulting patterns mined are typically easier to understand. Concept hierarchies are also useful for mining at multiple abstraction levels.
- Discretization, where the raw values of a numeric attribute (e.g., age) are replaced by interval labels (e.g., 0–10, 11–20, etc.) or conceptual labels (e.g., youth, adult, senior). The labels, in turn, can be recursively organized into higher-level concepts, resulting in a concept hierarchy for the numeric attribute.
- Fig. 4.14 shows a concept hierarchy for the attribute *price*. More than one concept hierarchy can be defined for the same attribute to accommodate the needs of various users.

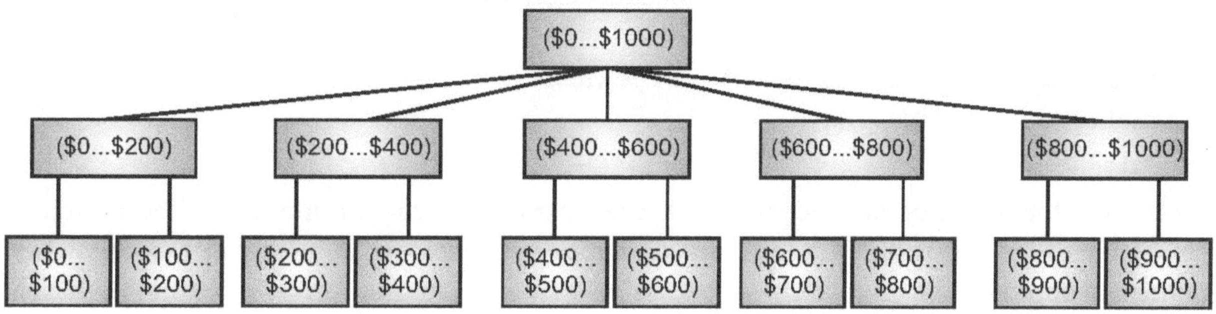

Fig. 4.14: A Concept Hierarchy for the Attribute Price, where an Interval $X ..... $Y) denotes the Range from $X (Exclusive) to $Y (Inclusive)

- The goal of discretization is to reduce the number of values a continuous variable assumes by grouping them into a number, b of intervals or bins.
- Discretization techniques can be categorized based on whether it uses class information or which direction it proceeds (i.e., top-down vs. bottom-up).

(i) Supervised Discretization: Here, discretization process uses class information.

(ii) Unsupervised Discretization: Here, discretization process not uses class information.

(iii) **Top-Down Discretization or Splittin:** Process starts by first finding one or a few points (called split points or cut points) to split the entire attribute range and then repeats this recursively on the resulting intervals.

(iv) **Bottom-Up Discretization or Merging:** Process starts by considering all of the continuous values as potential split-points, removes some by merging neighborhood values to form intervals and then recursively applies this process to the resulting intervals.

4.5 DATA CLEANING

- The noise and inconsistent data is removed in data cleaning. During data cleaning, we work on following kinds of data:

1. Missing Values:

- Data is not always available e.g., many tuples have no recorded value for several attributes, such as customer income in sales data. Missing data may be due to:
  (i) Equipment malfunction.
  (ii) Inconsistent with other recorded data and thus deleted.
  (iii) Data not entered due to misunderstanding.
  (iv) Certain data may not be considered important at the time of entry.
  (v) Not register history or changes of the data.
  (vi) Missing data may need to be inferred.
- Following are approaches through which we can handle the missing data:
  (i) Ignore the Tuple, usually done when class label is missing (assuming the tasks in classification-not effective when the percentage of missing values per attribute varies considerably).
  (ii) Fill in the missing value manually, is tedioustak and not feasible for human beings.
  (iii) Use a global constant to fill in the missing value, replace all missing attribute values by the same constant such as a label like "Unknown" or –1.
  (iv) Imputation uses the attribute mean to fill in the missing value, or use the attribute mean for all samples belonging to the same class to fill in the missing value.
  (v) Use the most probable value to fill in the missing value, inference-based such as Bayesian formula or decision tree.

2. Noisy Data:

- Noise is a random error or variance in a measured variable. Given a numeric attribute such as, say, price, how can we "smooth" out the data to remove the noise? Let's look at the following data smoothing techniques.
- Following are approaches through which we can handle the noisy data:
  (i) Binning Method:
- Binning methods first sort data by consulting its "neighborhood and then sorted values are distributed into a number of "buckets," or bins.
- In binning process we can partition the data following ways:
  (a) Equal-Width (Distance) Partitioning:
  - It divides the range into N intervals of equal size: For example, if A and B are the lowest and highest values of the attribute, the width of intervals will be:
    $W = (B - A)/N$.

- This approach is most straightforward, but outliers may dominate and Skewed data is not handled well.

Example:

Sorted data for price (in dollars): 4, 8, 15, 21, 21, 24, 25, 28, 34.

W = (B –A)/N = (34 – 4) / 3 = 10 Bin 1: 4 – 14, Bin2: 15 – 24, Bin 3: 25 – 34.

Equal - width (distance) partitioning:

Bin 1: 4, 8

Bin 2: 15, 21, 21, 24

Bin 3: 25, 28, 34

(b) Equal-Depth (Frequency) Partitioning:

- It divides the range into N intervals, each containing approximately same number of samples. It provides good data scaling but managing categorical attributes can be tricky.

Example:

Sorted data for price (in dollars): – 4, 8, 15, 21, 21, 24, 25, 28, 34.

In Partition into (equal-frequency) bins the data for price are first sorted and then partitioned into equal-frequency bins of size 3.

Equal-depth (frequency) partitioning:

Bin 1: 4, 8, 15

Bin 2: 21, 21, 24

Bin 3: 25, 28, 34

- In bin one can smooth the data by bin means, smooth by bin median, smooth by bin boundaries, etc.

Smoothing by Bin Means:

- In smoothing by bin means, each value in a bin is replaced by the mean value of the bin.

Example:

Sorted data for price (in dollars): – 4, 8, 15, 21, 21, 24, 25, 28, 34.

Bin a: 9, 9, 9

Bin b: 22, 22, 22

Bin c: 29, 29, 29

Smoothing by Bin Boundaries:

- In smoothing by bin boundaries, the minimum and maximum values in a given bin are identified as the bin boundaries.
- Each bin value is then replaced by the closest boundary value.

Sorted data for price (in dollars): – 4, 8, 15, 21, 21, 24, 25, 28, 34.

Bin a: 4, 4, 15

Bin b: 21, 21, 24

Bin c: 25, 25, 34

(ii) Clustering:

- Clustering can be used to detect outliers. For example, where similar values are organized into groups, or "clusters."
- Intuitively, values that fall outside of the set of clusters may be considered outliers.

(iii) Regression:

- Data smoothing can also be done by regression, a technique that conforms data values to a function. Linear regression involves finding the "best" line to fit two attributes (or variables) so that one attribute can be used to predict the other.
- Multiple linear regression is an extension of linear regression, where more than two attributes are involved and the data are fit to a multidimensional surface.

4.5.1 Data Cleaning as a Process

- Upto now, under data cleaning we have seen different techniques for handling missing data and for smoothing data. Missing values, noise, outliers and inconsistencies all these contribute to inaccurate data.
- An outlier is a data object that deviates significantly from the rest of the objects, as if it were generated by a different mechanism.
- The first step in data cleaning as a process is discrepancy detection. Discrepancies can be caused by several factors,
  1. Poor data entry by human beings or certain data may not be considered important at the time of entry.
  2. Inconsistent with other recorded data or inconsistencies due to data integration.
  3. Data not entered due to misunderstanding.
  4. Not register history or changes of the data.
  5. Errors in instrumentation devices that record data and system errors.
  6. Errors can also occur when the data are (inadequately) used for purposes other than originally intended.
  7. Experimental errors (data extraction or experiment planning/executing errors).
- As there can be many factors for discrepancy how one can proceed further? In order to detect the discrepancies in data at hand there are different ways.

Using Metadata:

- As a starting point, use any knowledge you may already have regarding properties of the data. Such knowledge or "data about data" is referred to as metadata.
- To grasp data trends and identify anomalies get the answers of following questions using metadata.
  1. What are the data type and domain of each attribute?
  2. What are the acceptable values for each attribute?
  3. Are there any known dependencies between attributes?
- Once, we will get the data type and acceptable values from metadata then find out the answer of following:
  1. Find the mean, median, and mode values: From this we will come to know the data distribution around the mean and can see whether the data symmetric or skewed (imbalance).
  2. What is the range of values?: From this we can interpret that whether all values fall within the expected range or note.
  3. What is the standard deviation of each attribute? : Values that are more than two standard deviations away from the mean for a given attribute may be flagged as potential outliers.

- From all these, we may find noise, outliers, and unusual values that need investigation.

Looking for Inconsistency:

- As a data analyst, we should be on the lookout for the inconsistent use of codes and any inconsistent data representations (e.g., "2010/12/25" and "25/12/2010" for date).

Checking of Data Corresponding to Rule:

- The data should also be examined regarding unique rules, consecutive rules and null rules.
    1. A **unique rule** says that each value of the given attribute must be different from all other values for that attribute. (e.g. record id)
    2. A **consecutive rule** says that there can be no missing values between the lowest and highest values for the attribute, and that all values must also be unique (e.g., as in check numbers).
    3. A **null rule** specifies the use of blanks, question marks, special characters, or other strings that may indicate the null condition. (e.g., where a value for a given attribute is not available)

Using Commercial Tools:

- There are a number of different commercial tools that can help in the data cleaning and data transformation. Some tools are given below:
    1. **Data Scrubbing Tools** use simple domain knowledge to detect errors and make corrections in the data. These tools rely on parsing and fuzzy matching techniques when cleaning data from multiple sources. For example knowledge of postal addresses and spell-checking.
    2. **Data Auditing Tools** find discrepancies by analyzing the data to discover rules and relationships, and detecting data that violate such conditions, e.g. clustering to identify outliers.
    3. **Data Migration Tools** these tools help in data transformation and allow simple transformations to be specified such as to replace the string "rollno" by "id".
    4. **ETL (Extraction/Transformation/Loading) tools** also help in data transformation andallow users to specify transforms through a Graphical User Interface (GUI).
- These tools typically support only a restricted set of transforms hence need to write custom code/scripts for data cleaning process.

Outlier Detection Methods:

- Some of the most popular methods for outlier detection are explain below:
    1. **Extreme Value Analysis:** This is the most basic form of outlier detection and only good for 1-dimension data. In these types of analysis, it is assumed that values which are too large or too small are outliers. Z-test and Student's t-test are examples of these statistical methods. These are good heuristics for initial analysis of data but they don't have much value in multivariate settings. They can be used as final steps for interpreting outputs of other outlier detection methods.
    2. **Probabilistic and Statistical Models:** These models assume specific distributions for data. Then using the Expectation-Maximization (EM) methods they estimate the parameters of the model. Finally, they calculate probability of membership of each data point to calculated distribution. The points with low probability of membership are marked as outliers.
    3. **Linear Models:** These methods model the data into a lower dimensional sub-spaces with the use of linear correlations. Then the distance of each data point to plane that fits the sub-space is

being calculated. This distance is used to find outliers. PCA (Principal Component Analysis) is an example of linear models for anomaly detection.

4. **Proximity-based Models:** The idea with these methods is to model outliers as points which are isolated from rest of observations. The most common ways of defining proximity for outlier analysis are as follows:
   (i) **Cluster Analysis:** The non-membership of a data point in any cluster, its distance from other clusters, and the size of the closest cluster, are used as criteria in order to compute the outlier score. The clustering problem has a complementary relationship to the outlier detection problem, in which points either belong to clusters or outliers.
   (ii) **Distance Based Analysis:** The distance of a data point to its k-nearest neighbor (or other variant) is used in order to define proximity. Data points with large k-nearest neighbor distances are defined as outliers. Distance-based algorithms typically perform the analysis at a much more detailed granularity than the other two methods. On the other hand, this greater granularity often comes at a significant computational cost.
   (iii) **Density Based Analysis:** The number of other points within a specified local region (grid region or distance-based region) of a data point, is used in order to define local density. These local density values may be converted into outlier scores. Other kernel-based methods or statistical methods for density estimation may also be used. The major difference between clustering and density-based methods is that clustering methods partition the data points, whereas density based methods partition the data space.
5. **Information Theoretic Models:** The idea of these methods is the fact that outliers increase the minimum code length to describe a data set.
6. **High-Dimensional Outlier Detection:** Specific methods to handle high dimensional sparse data.

4.5.2 Data Mining Technology and its Relation to Data Warehousing

- Data mining is a very recently developed subject area that deals with meaningful information extraction from large volumes of related or unrelated data gathered from various sources for the purpose of any possible future use.
- Data mining, the extraction of hidden predictive information from large databases, is a powerful new technology with great potential to help companies focus on the most important information in their data warehouses.
- Data mining tools predict future trends and behaviors, allowing businesses to make proactive, knowledge-driven decisions. The automated, prospective analyses offered by data mining move beyond the analyses of past events provided by retrospective tools typical of decision support systems.
- Data mining as the process of discovering meaningful new correlations, patterns, and trends by digging into (mining) large amounts of data stored in warehouses, using Artificial Intelligence (AI) and statistical and mathematical techniques.
- Data mining is the process of extracting previously unknown, valid and actionable information from large data (as transaction data or database or data warehouse) and then using the information so derived to make crucial business and strategic decisions. Data mining may lead to knowledge discovery in the data mined upon (Piatetsky and Frawley, 1991).

* The mined information may be in terms of any associations or any other relations between the data items in the data. But it is essential that such associations or relationships identified by mining process be verifiable (i.e., valid), actionable (i.e., can be causing some action), and of course, be previously unknown, (See Fig. 4.15).

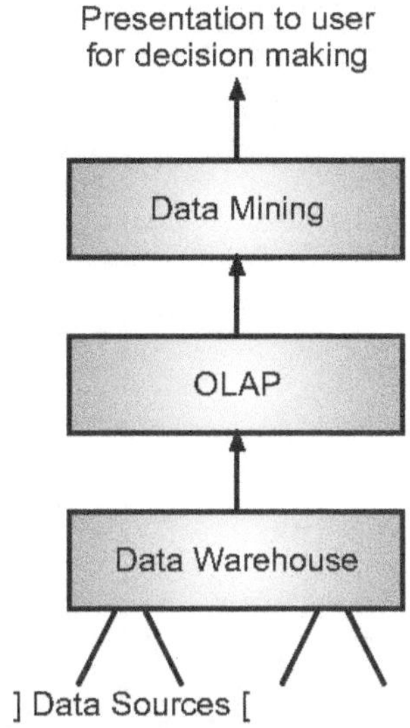

Fig. 4.15: The Data Mining Hierarchy in Business Decision Support

Comparison between Data Mining and Data Warehouse:

Sr. No.	Data Mining	Data Warehouse
1.	Data mining is the process of analyzing unknown patterns of data.	A data warehouse is used to integrate data from multiple sources and then combine it into a single database.
2.	Data mining techniques are applied on data warehouse in order to discover useful patterns.	It provides the organization a mechanism to store huge amount of data.
3.	Data mining is the process of analyzing unknown patterns of data.	Data warehousing is the process of pooling all relevant data together.
4.	Data mining is a broad set of activities used to uncover patterns, and give meaning to this data.	Data warehouse is the repository to store data.
5.	As Facebook stores all the data in central aggregate database, now users can extract meaningful data patterns from it. That is, users can see the ads, get friends suggestions relevant to them, etc. This implies the data mining phase.	For example, Facebook gathers (collects) all user's data such as his/her friends, likes, and messages, notifications. etc., and then stores them into a central repository.
6.	This process is always carried out after data warehousing process because it needs compiled data in order to extract useful patterns.	This process must take place before the data mining process because it compiles and organizes the data into a common database.
7.	Low maintenance.	Data warehouses has high maintenance.

Contd....

Sr. No.	Data Mining	Data Warehouse
8.	After successful initial queries, users may ask more complicated queries which would increase the workload.	Data Warehouse (DW) is complicated to implement and maintain.
9.	The data mining methods are cost-effective and efficient compares to other statistical data applications.	Data warehouse's responsibility is to simplify every type of business data. Most of the work that will be done on user's part is inputting the raw data.
10.	Data mining helps to generate actionable strategies built on data insights.	Once you input any information into Data warehouse system, you will unlikely to lose track of this data again. You need to conduct a quick search, helps you to find the right statistic information.
11.	Data is analyzed regularly in data mining.	Data is stored periodically in DW.

Practice Questions

1. What is data mining? Give advantages of data mining.
2. Explain steps of knowledge discovery process.
3. Explain data mining tasks in detail.
4. Explain what type of data can be mined?
5. Explain challenges and issues in data mining.
6. What is data object? Explain different types of attributes.
7. Explain the steps involved in data Preprocessing.
8. Explain data transformation and its techniques.
9. Explain data reduction and its techniques.
10. Explain data cleaning as a process.
11. Give difference between data mining and data warehouse.

❖ ❖ ❖

5... Mining Frequent Patterns and Cluster Analysis

Chapter Outcomes...

- Define the itemsets for the given data.
- Describe the given association rules.
- Explain clustering methods for the given data.
- Analyze Apriori algorithm for the given data.

Learning Objectives...

- To understand Basic Concepts in Mining Frequent Patterns
- To learn Frequent Itemsets Mining Methods
- To study Concepts in Cluster Analysis
- To understand Basic Clustering Methods

5.0 INTRODUCTION

- Frequent patterns, as the name suggests, are patterns that occur frequently in data. A frequent item set typically refers to a set of items that often appear together in a transactional data set.
- For example, a set of items, such as milk and bread, that appear frequently together in a transaction data set is a frequent itemset.
- A typical example of frequent itemset mining is market basket analysis. This process analyzes customer buying habits by finding associations between the different items that customers place in their "shopping baskets".
- The discovery of these associations can help retailers develop marketing strategies by gaining insight into which items are frequently purchased together by customers. Cluster analysis deals with separating data into groups whose identities are not known in advance.
- Cluster is a group of objects that belongs to the same class. In other words, similar objects are grouped in one cluster and dissimilar objects are grouped in another cluster.
- Clustering is the process of making a group of abstract objects into classes of similar objects. Cluster analysis deals with separating data into groups whose identities are not known in advance.
- Cluster analysis or clustering is the task of grouping a set of objects in such a way that objects in the same group (called a cluster) are more similar (in some sense) to each other than to those in other groups (clusters).
- The purpose of clusetering techniques is to detect similar subgroups among a large collection of cases and to assign those observations to the clusters.

- Frequent pattern mining is a data mining part with the objective of extracting frequent itemsets from a database. Frequent itemsets play an essential role in many data mining tasks and are related to interesting patterns in data, such as Association Rules.
- Association analysis is used for finding and describing relationships between different items in large data sets.
- Association analysis is one of the functionality of data mining which discovers the association relationships among huge amounts of data. Association analysis measures the strength of co-occurrence between one item and another
- Association analysis is uncovering data relationships and using the asset to gain competitive advantage. It is a means to discover relationships in large data sets.
- Hidden data relationships will be expressed as a collection of association rules and frequent item sets with association analysis.
- While association rules suggest a strong relationship that exists between two items, frequent items are a collection of items that frequently occur together.
- Association analysis helps us in following ways:
  1. Increase our average sales by discounting the correct item revealed in the association analysis;
  2. Gain competitive customer insights by knowing how the products are associated in different segments;
  3. Differentiate discount offers based on market basket analysis.
- Association technique aims to find all relations among data in such a manner that the presence of one set of items in a transaction implies the other items. This is represented in the form of association rule.
- Association rule mining finds interesting associations and/or correlation relationships among large sets of such data items. Association rules show attribute value conditions that occur frequently together in a given dataset.

  $A \rightarrow B$, where A and B are data sets.
- It means that the transaction which tends to contain A also tends to contain B. However, there are two measures which describe the rule's strength, namely support and confidence.
  1. The **Support** is the percentage of transactions that contains the probability $P(A \cup B)$. Support measures how often items occur together, as a percentage of the total transactions.
  2. The **Confidence** is the percentage of transactions containing both A and B, that is, $P(B \mid A)$. Confidence measures how much a particular item is dependent on another.
- For example, consider an association rule milk → bread [Support=8%, Confidence=80%. A support of 8% means that from all the transactions only 8% purchased milk and bread together]. On the other hand, a confidence of 80% means that there is a probability that 80% will purchase both items together.
- Typically, association rules are strong if they satisfy both minimum support threshold and minimum confidence threshold. Such thresholds are set by users or domain experts.

5.1 MINING FREQUENT PATTERN (BASIC CONCEPT)

- A frequent pattern is a pattern (item sets, sub-sequences, sub-graphs etc.) that occurs frequently in a data set. There are many kinds of frequent patterns, including itemsets, sub-sequences (sequential) and sub-structures.
- A frequent itemset typically refers to a set of items that frequently appear together in a transactional data set, such as milk and bread.

- A frequently occurring subsequence, such as the pattern that customers tend to purchase first a PC, followed by a digital camera, and then a memory card, is a (frequent) sequential pattern.
- A sub-structure can refer to different structural forms, such as graphs, trees, or lattices, which may be combined with item sets or sub sequences.
- If a sub-structure occurs frequently, it is called a (frequent) structured pattern. Mining frequent patterns leads to the discovery of interesting associations and correlations within data.

5.1.1 Market Basket Analysis

- Frequent pattern mining is also called as association rule mining.
- It is an analytical process that finds frequent patterns, associations, or causal structures from data sets found in various kinds of databases such as relational databases, transactional databases, and other data repositories.
- Association rule mining searches for interesting relationships among items in a given dataset. The strengths of association rule analysis are:
  1. It produces clear and understandable results.
  2. It supports undirected data mining.
  3. It works on variable-length data.
  4. The computations it uses are simple to understandable.

Example:

- Suppose, a marketing manager of Electronic shop, would like to determine which items are frequently purchased together within the same transactions.
- An example of such a rule,

  buys (X; "computer") → buys(X; "Antivirus software") [support = 1%; confidence = 50%]

  where, X is a variable representing a customer.
- Here, support and confidence are two measures of rule interestingness.
- A Confidence, or Certainty, of 50% means that if a customer buys a computer, there is a 50% chance that customer will buy antivirus software as well.
- A 1% Support means that 1% of all of the transactions under analysis showed that computer and antivirus software were purchased together. This association rule involves a single attribute or predicate (i.e., buys) that repeats.
- Association rules that contain a single predicate are referred to as single-dimensional association rules. Dropping the predicate notation, the above rule can be written simply as

  "Computer → antivirus software [1%, 50%]".
- Suppose, that we are given the Electronic store relational database relating to purchases. A data mining system may find association rules like,

  `age (X, "20:::29")^income(X, "20K:::29K") →buys(X, "Laptop") [support = 2%, confidence = 60%]`
- The rule indicates that of the customers under study, 2% are 20 to29 years of age with an income of 20,000 to 29,000 and have purchased a laptop at Electronic store. There is a 60% probability that a customer in this age and income group will purchase a laptop.
- Note that there is an association between more than one attribute, or predicate (i.e., age, income, and buys). Adopting the terminology used in multidimensional databases, where each attribute is referred to as a dimension, the above rule can be referred to as a multidimensional association rule.
- Typically, association rules are considered interesting if they satisfy both a minimum support threshold and a minimum confidence threshold.

- Additional analysis can be performed to uncover interesting statistical correlations between associated attribute-value pairs.

Association Rule Metrics/Measures:

- Various metrics are in place to help us understand the strength of association between these two itemsets.

1. **Support:** The support of a rule $x \to y$ (where x and y are each items/events etc.) is defined as the proportion of transactions in the data set which contain the item set x as well as y. So,

$$\text{Support } (x \to y) = \frac{\text{Number of transactions which contain the item set x and y}}{\text{Total number of transactions}}$$

Whereas,

$$\text{Support } (x) = \frac{\text{Number of transactions which contain the item set x}}{\text{Total number of transactions}}$$

2. **Confidence:** The confidence of a rule $x \to y$ is defined as:

$$\text{Confidence } (x \to y) = \frac{\text{Support } (x \to y)}{\text{Support } (x)}$$

- So, it is the ratio of the number of transactions that include all items in the consequent (y in this case), as well as the antecedent (x in this case) to the number of transactions that include all items in the antecedent (x in this case).
- In the table below, Support (milk $\to$ bread) = 0.4 means milk and bread are purchased together occur in 40% of all transactions. Confidence (milk $\to$ bread) = 0.5 means that if there are 100 transactions containing milk then there will be 50 that will also contain bread.

TID	Milk	Bread	Butter	Beer
1	1	0	1	1
2	1	1	1	0
3	0	1	1	0
4	1	0	0	1
5	1	1	1	1

Lift:

- Lift measures dependency between X and Y.

$$\text{Lift } (x \to y) = \frac{\text{Support } (x \to y)}{\text{Support } (x) \times \text{Support } (y)} = \frac{\text{Confidence } (x \to y)}{\text{Support } (y)}$$

- The numerator for lift is the proportion of transactions where x and y occur jointly. The denominator is an estimate of the expected joint occurrence of x and y, assuming that they occur independently.
- A lift value of 1 indicates that x and y jointly occur in transactions with the frequency that would be expected by chance alone.
- The preferred values are much larger or smaller than 1, whereby values less than 1 mean x and y are negatively correlated and greater values indicate positive correlation.
- Lift is vulnerable to noise in small datasets, because infrequent itemset can have very high lift values.

Example:

- In 70% of the circumstances, when customers buy paneer, they also buy milk. This shows the association between paneer and milk. We can represent it as:

  paneer$\to$ milk| 70%

- Association Rules find all sets of items (itemsets) that have support **greater** than the minimum support and then using the large itemsets to generate the desired rules that have **confidence** greater than the minimum confidence.
- The **lift** of a rule is the ratio of the observed support to that expected if X and Y were independent. A typical and widely used example of association rules application is market basket analysis.

Rule	Support	Confidence	Lift
A ⇒ D	2/5	2/3	10/9
C ⇒ A	2/5	2/4	5/6
A ⇒ V	2/5	2/3	5/6
B & C ⇒ D	1/5	1/3	5/9

Fig. 5.1

5.1.2 Frequent Itemset, Closed Itemset and Association Rules

- A set of items that frequently appear together in a transactional data set is called as **frequent itemset,** such as milk and bread.
- **Maximal Frequent Itemset** says that an itemset is maximal frequent if none of its immediate supersets is frequent.
- **Closed Frequent Itemset** says that an itemset is closed if none of its immediate supersets has the same support as that of the itemset.
- It is important to point out the relationship between frequent itemsets, closed frequent itemsets and maximal frequent itemsets.
- As mentioned earlier closed and maximal frequent itemsets are subsets of frequent itemsets but maximal frequent itemsets are a more compact representation because it is a subset of closed frequent itemsets.
- The Fig. 5.2 shows the relationship between these three types of itemsets.

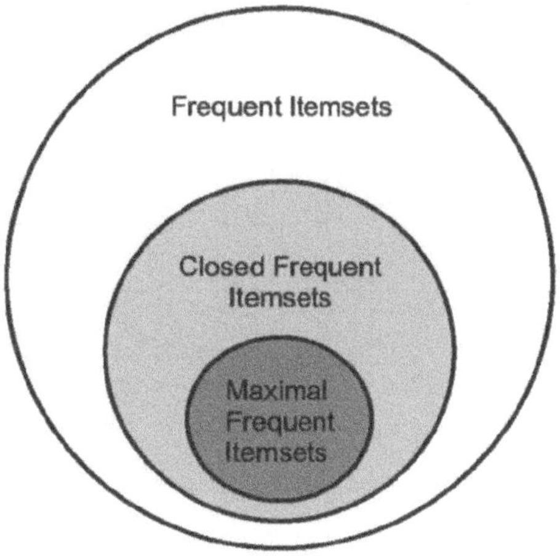

Fig. 5.2

- Closed frequent itemsets are more widely used than maximal frequent itemset because when efficiency is more important that space, they provide us with the support of the subsets so no additional pass is needed to find this information.
- The analytical process that finds frequent itemset and associations from data sets is called frequent pattern mining or association rule mining.
- Consider following example is used to understand the concept of frequent itemset, closed itemset and maximal itemset.

- **Example:** Consider the given dataset "Shopping" with 6 transactions, each transaction consist of items which were purchase together.

Transaction ID	Items
1	A,B,C,E
2	A,C,D,E
3	B,C,E
4	A,C,D,E
5	C,D,E
6	A,D,E

Let's say min_support=0.5. This is fulfilled if min_support_count>= 3.

- Frequent item set X ∈ FX ∈ F is maximal if it does not have any frequent supersets.
- Frequent item set X ∈ F is closed if it has no superset with the same frequency.

Find Frequent Item Set:

- A frequent itemset is simply a set of items occurring a certain percentage of the time. In a dataset , a itemset is considered frequent if its frequency/occurrence is equal or more than on min_support % or min_support_count.
- Following table is showing the all frequent item set on shopping dataset.

Table 5.1 : Frequent itemsets

Itemsets	Frequency/Occurrence	Decision
1-itemset	{A} = 4	Frequent.
	{B} = 2	Not frequent => ignore.
	{C} = 5	Frequent.
	{D} = 4	Frequent.
	{E} = 6	Frequent.
2-itemset	{A,B} = 1	Not frequent => ignore.
	{A,C} = 3	Frequent.
	{A,D} = 3	Frequent.
	{A,E} = 4	Frequent.
	{B,C} = 2	Not frequent => ignore.
	{B,D} = 0	Not frequent => ignore.
	{B,E} = 2	Not frequent => ignore.
	{C,D} = 3	Frequent.
	{C,E} = 5	Frequent.
	{D,E} = 4	Frequent.

Itemsets	Frequency/Occurrence	Decision
3-itemset	{A,B,C} = 1	Not frequent => ignore.
	{A,B,D} = 0	Not frequent => ignore.
	{A,B,E} = 1	Not frequent => ignore.
	{A,C,D} = 2	Not frequent => ignore.
	{A,C,E} = 3	Frequent
	{A,D,E} = 3	Frequent
	{B,C,D} = 0	Not frequent => ignore
	{B,C,E} = 2	Not frequent => ignore
	{C,D,E} = 3	Frequent
4-itemset	{A,B,C,D} = 0	Not frequent => ignore
	{A,B,C,E} = 1	Not frequent => ignore
	{B,C,D,E} = 0	Not frequent => ignore

Finding Closed Itemset:

- From Table 5.1 consider all the item sets which are frequent and then check for the property of closed itemset i.e., Frequent item set X ∊ F is closed if it has no superset with the same frequency.
- Following table is showing the all closed frequent item set on shopping dataset.

Table 5.2: Closed itemsets

Item sets	Frequency/Occurrence	Closed Decision
1-itemset	{A} = 4	Not closed due to {A,E}as having same frequency.
	{C} = 5	Not closed due to {C,E} as having same frequency.
	{D} = 4	Not closed due to {D,E} as having same frequency.
	{E} = 6	Closed.
2-itemset	{A,C} = 3	Not closed due to {A,C,E} as having same frequency.
	{A,D} = 3	Not closed due to {A,D,E} as having same frequency.
	{A,E} = 4	Closed.
	{C,D} = 3	Not closed due to {C,D,E} as having same frequency.
	{C,E} = 5	Closed.
	{D,E} = 4	Closed.
3-itemset	{A,C,E} = 3	Not closed as no superset with the same frequency.
	{A,D,E} = 3	Not closed as no superset with the same frequency.
	{C,D,E} = 3	Not closed as no superset with the same frequency.

Finding Maximal Itemset

- From Table 5.1 consider all the item sets which are frequent and then check for the property of maximal itemset i.e., frequent item set X ∊ FX ∊ F is maximal if it does not have any frequent supersets.

- Following table is showing the all maximal frequent item set on shopping Dataset.

Table 5.3 : Maximal itemsets

Item Sets	Frequency/Occurrence	Decision
1-itemset	{A} = 4	Not Maximal due to its frequent superset.
	{C} = 5	Not Maximal frequent due to its frequent superset.
	{D} = 4	Not Maximal frequent due to its frequent superset.
	{E} = 6	Not Maximal frequent due to its frequent superset.
2-itemset	{A,C} = 3	Not Maximal frequent due to its frequent superset.
	{A,D} = 3	Not Maximal frequent due to its frequent superset.
	{A,E} = 4	Not Maximal frequent due to its frequent superset.
	{C,D} = 3	Not Maximal frequent due to its frequent superset.
	{C,E} = 5	Not Maximal frequent due to its frequent superset.
	{D,E} = 4	Not Maximal frequent due to its frequent superset.
3-itemset	{A,C,E} = 3	Maximal frequent.
	{A,D,E} = 3	Maximal Frequent.
	{C,D,E} = 3	Maximal Frequent.

- Association rules are the statements which are used to find the relationships between unrelated data in a database. These rules are useful for analyzing and predicting customer behavior.
- Support and Confidence are two methods for generating the association rules. The frequent items are calculated by support threshold and confidence threshold. The values for these thresholds are predefined by the users.
- Mining association rules consist of following two-step approach:
  1. **Frequent Itemset Generation:** Generate all itemsets whose support ≥ minsup.
  2. **Rule Generation:** Generate high confidence rules from each frequent itemset, where each rule is a binary partitioning of a frequent itemset.

5.2 FREQUENT ITEMSET MINING METHODS

- Several algorithms for generating rules have been used in the research work carried out by various authors. Here, we will study the Apriori Algorithm and FP Growth algorithm for generating the frequent itemsets. Here, we see the Apriori algorithm in detail.
- Apriori algorithm finds interesting association along with a huge set of data items. The association rule mining problem was firstly given by Apriori algorithm by Rakesh Agrawal and Ramakrishnan Srikant in 1994 in the following manner:

  Let I = $\{I_1, I_2 ...... I_m\}$, m ∈ I be a set of m different attributes, T be the transaction that covers a set of items and D be a database. A rule is a relationship in the form of X=>Y, where X and Y are called itemsets.

  For example, it could be functional for the video store manager to recognize what movies are frequently borrowed together or if there is a correlation between renting a certain type of movies or buying popcorn.

5.1.1 Apriori Algorithm (Finding Frequent Itemset using Candidate Generation)

- Apriori algorithm is the most basic and well-known algorithm to find frequent itemsets in a transactional database.

- The name of the algorithm is based on the fact that the algorithm uses prior knowledge of frequent itemset properties. It is a classic algorithm for learning association rules.
- Apriori algorithm is easy to execute and very simple is used to mine all frequent itemsets in database.
- The algorithm makes many searches in database to find frequent itemsets where k itemsets are used to generate k + 1 itemsets. Each k itemset must be greater than or equal to minimum support threshold to be frequency.
- Otherwise, it is called candidate itemsets. In the first, the algorithm scan database to find frequency of 1 itemsets that contains only one item by counting each item in database.
- The frequency of 1 itemsets is used to find the itemsets in 2 itemsets which in turn is used to find 3 itemsets and so on until there are not any more k itemsets. If an itemset is not frequent, any large subset from it is also non-frequent; this condition prune from search space in database.
- Apriori algorithm uses Apriori property which specify that all subsets of a frequent itemset must also be frequent. This property belongs to a special category of properties called antimonotonicity in the sense that if a set cannot pass a test, all of its supersets will fail the same test as well.
- It is called antimonotonicity because the property is monotonic in the context of failing a test.

Algorithm for Apriori:

Input: D, database.
min_sup: Minimum Support Threshold.

Output: L, Frequent itemsets in database.

1. Scan the database to determine the support of each one-itemset, compare it with min_sup and get the frequent one-itemset, (L_1).
2. Use L_{K-1} property, Join L_{K-1} to find the candidate k itemset.
3. Scan the database to find the support of each candidate k-itemset, compare it with min_sup and get the frequent K-itemset.
4. Repeat the Steps 2 to 3 until candidate itemset is null. If null, generate all subsets for each frequent itemset.

- Consider, total number of transactions is 15 and Min Support =20%.

TID	List of Items
1	1, 5, 6, 8
2	2, 4, 8
3	4, 5, 7
4	2, 3
5	5, 6, 7
6	2, 3, 4
7	2, 6, 7, 9
8	5
9	8
10	3, 5, 7
11	3, 5, 7
12	5, 6, 8
13	2, 4, 6, 7
14	1, 3, 5, 7
15	2, 3, 9

Calculate Minimum Support:

- First should calculate the minimum SupportCount/threshold. Question says minimum support should be 20%. It calculate as follows:

  Minimum support count$(20/100 \times 15) = 3$.

  Scan 1: Calculate SupportCount for frequency itmset (C_1)

Itemset	SupportCount
1	2
2	6
3	6
4	4
5	8
6	5
7	7
8	4
9	2

Prune 1: Prune C_1 by comparing with min, SupportCount i.e. 3 and keep those items in L_1 which > 3 support count.

Itemset	SupportCount
2	6
3	6
4	4
5	8
6	5
7	7
8	4

Scan 2: Calculate SupportCount for frequent two itemset (C_2) using L_1.

Itemset	SupportCount	Itemset	Support Count
{2, 3}	3	{4, 5}	1
{2, 4}	3	{4, 6}	1
{2, 5}	0	{4, 7}	2
{2, 6}	2	{4, 8}	1
{2, 7}	2	{5, 6}	3
{2, 8}	1	{5, 7}	5
{3, 4}	1	{5, 8}	2
{3, 5}	3	{6, 7}	3
{3, 6}	0	{6, 8}	2
{3, 7}	3	{7, 8}	0
{3, 8}	0		

Prune 2: Prune C_2 by comparing with min, SupportCount i.e., 3. and keep those items in L_2 which > 3 SupportCount.

Itemset	SupportCount
{2, 3}	3
{2, 4}	3
{3, 5}	3
{3, 7}	3
{5, 6}	3
{5, 7}	5
{6, 7}	3

Scan 3: Calculate SupportCount for frequent three itmeset (C_3) using L_2.

Itemset	SupportCount
{2, 3, 4}	1
{3, 5, 7}	3
{5, 6, 7}	1

Prune 3: Prune C_3 by comparing with min, SupportCount i.e. three itemset (C_3) in L_3 which > 3 SupportCount.

Itemset	SupportCount
{3, 5, 7}	3

At the end {3, 5, 7} represent a frequent itemset in transaction.

Example: For Apriori algorithm.

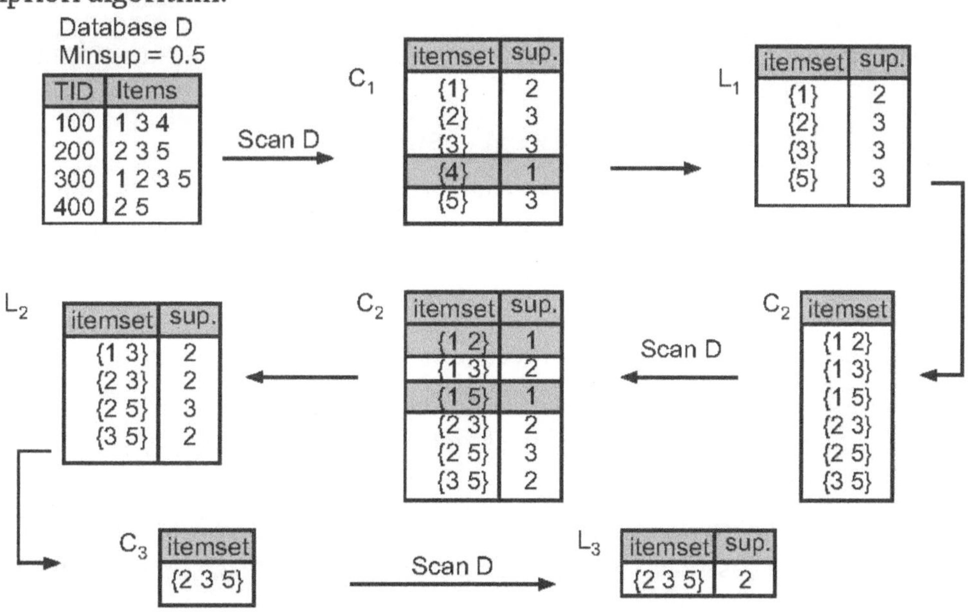

Fig. 5.3: Apriori Algorithm Example

- The weaknesses of association rule are:
  1. It requires exponentially more computational effort as the problem size grows.
  2. It has a limited support for attributes on the data.
  3. It is difficult to determine the right number of items.

5.3 GENERATING ASSOCIATION RULES FROM FREQUENT ITEMSETS

- Once, the frequent itemsets are generated, identifying rules out of them is comparatively very easy. Rules are formed by binary partition of each itemset.
- Since, only relevant rules are of interest, the question arises how to measure this relevance. The most common way is by using confidence. The confidence of a rule, $X \Rightarrow Y$, is known as the conditional probability of a transaction containing Y given that it contains X. This can be calculated according to this formula: Confidence $(X \Rightarrow Y) = Sup(X \cup Y)/Sup(X)$.
- Given two disjoint itemsets X and Y. An implication expression of the form $X \Rightarrow Y$ is referred to as an association rule with a minimum support level minsup and a minimum confidence level minconf, if both following criteria are satisfied:
  1. $Sup(X \cup Y) \geq minsup$
  2. $Conf(X \Rightarrow Y) \geq minconf$
- Since, only rules of certain relevance are of interest, similar to minsup in frequent itemset mining, a specific minimum confidence threshold is needed to generate only the most relevant rules.
- For generation of any rule, first thing is to determine the frequent itemset. Given a frequent itemset L, find all non-empty subsets $f \in L$ such that $f \rightarrow L - f$ satisfies the minimum confidence requirement
- If {A,B,C,D} is a frequent itemset, then possible candidate rules are:

  $ABC \rightarrow D$, $ABD \rightarrow C$, $ACD \rightarrow B$, $BCD \rightarrow A$, $A \rightarrow BCD$, $B \rightarrow ACD$, $C \rightarrow ABD$, $D \rightarrow ABC$

  $AB \rightarrow CD$, $AC \rightarrow BD$, $AD \rightarrow BC$, $BC \rightarrow AD$, $BD \rightarrow AC$, $CD \rightarrow AB$.
- If $|L| = k$, then there are $2^k - 2$ candidate association rules (ignoring $L \rightarrow \phi$ and $\phi \rightarrow L$). In above case $|L|=4$ then there are $2^4 - 2 = 14$ subsets.
- In general, confidence does not have an anti-monotone property (as already explained in Apriori algorithm) $c(ABC \rightarrow D)$ can be larger or smaller than $c(AB \rightarrow D)$.
- But confidence of rules generated from the same itemset have an anti-monotone property for example,

  $$L = \{A, B, C, D\} : c(ABC \rightarrow D) \geq c(AB \rightarrow CD) \geq c(A \rightarrow BCD)$$
- If we will follow the antimonotonic property then we can prune most of the low confidence rules. We start with a frequent itemset {A,B,C,D} and start forming rules with just one consequent. Remove the rules failing to satisfy the minconf condition.
- Now, start forming rules using a combination of consequents from the remaining ones. Keep repeating until only one item is left on antecedent. This process has to be done for all frequent itemsets.
- In Apriori algorithm, at the end of example, we get a frequent itemset X = {3, 5, 7} but the task of generation of rule is not still achieved.
- Association rules can be generated from X. The non-empty subsets of X are {3, 5, 7}, {3, 5}, {5, 7}, {3, 7}, {3}, {5} and {7}. The resulting association rules are as shown below, each listed with its confidence.

Association Rules	Confidence = $\frac{\text{Sub (X} \cup \text{Y)}}{\text{Sup (X)}}$
$\{3, 5\} \rightarrow 7$	3/3 = 100%
$\{3, 7\} \rightarrow 5$	3/3 = 100%
$\{5, 7\} \rightarrow 3$	3/5 = 60%
$3 \rightarrow \{5, 7\}$	3/6 = 50%
$5 \rightarrow \{3, 7\}$	3/8 = 37.5%
$7 \rightarrow \{3, 5\}$	3/7 = 42.8%

- Now as per confidence value we can select the rule from frequent time set. For example, confidence threshold is 75 then two rules will be generated from frequent itemset {3, 5, 7}.

  $\{3, 5\} \rightarrow 7$

  $\{3, 7\} \rightarrow 5$

5.4 WHAT IS CLUSTER ANALYSIS?

- Clustering is the process of grouping a set of data objects into multiple groups/clusters so that objects within a cluster have high similarity, but are very dissimilar to objects in other clusters.
- Clustering is an unsupervised machine learning algorithm that divides a data into meaningful sub-groups, called clusters.
- The subgroups are chosen such that the intra-cluster differences are minimized and the inter-cluster differences are maximized.
- Clustering analysis has been an emerging research issue in data mining due its variety of applications.
- With the advent of many data clustering algorithms in the recent few years and its extensive use in wide variety of applications, including image processing, computational biology, mobile communication, medicine and economics, has lead to the popularity of this algorithms.
- Cluster analysis is very helpful to find patterns of data, studying the properties of each cluster and then inferring results from them.
- For doing so, there are various clustering algorithms such as partitioning methods, hierarchical methods, density-based methods, etc.
- Different types of clustering algorithms are suited to different types of datasets and different purposes. The main functions of clustering algorithm is to place similar points in the same cluster while placing dissimilar points in different clusters.
- Cluster analysis is the process of partitioning a set of data objects (or observations) into subsets. Each subset is a cluster, such that objects in a cluster are similar to one another, yet dissimilar to objects in other clusters.
- The set of clusters resulting from a cluster analysis can be referred to as a clustering. In this context, different clustering methods may generate different clusterings on the same data set.
- The partitioning is not performed by humans, but by the clustering algorithm. Hence, clustering is useful in that it can lead to the discovery of previously unknown groups within the data.

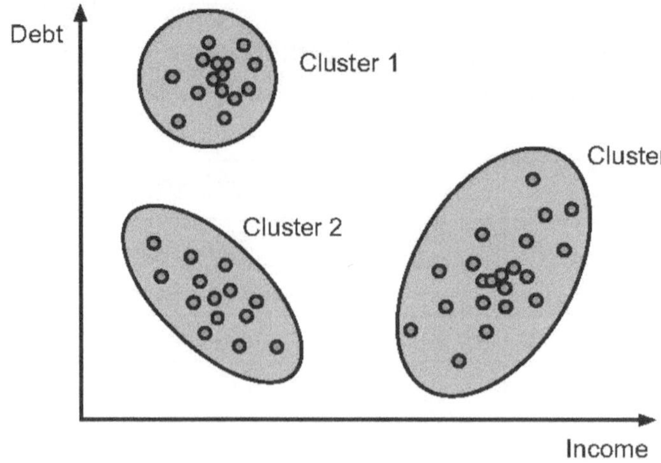

Fig. 5.4 : Clustering

- It is different from classification in a way that classification is supervised learning and clustering is unsupervised learning.
- Dissimilarities and similarities are assessed based on the attribute values describing the objects and often involve distance measures.

Measure of Similarity:

- Similarity is quantity that reflects the strength of relationship between two objects or two features. Similarity is important measure used in most of clustering algorithms.
- The range of similarity measure is usually having range of either –1 to +1 or normalized into 0 to 1.

Example:

	Object A	Object B
Feature1	0	7
Feature2	3	6
Feature3	4	3
Feature4	5	–1

- Here, we are representing the two objects based on its features. Point A has coordinate (0, 3, 4, 5) and point B has coordinate (7, 6, 3, –1). Dissimilarity (or similarity) between the two objects are based on these coordinates.
- There are various distance formula which can be used a similarity measure.

Euclidean Distance:

- Euclidean Distance is the most common use of distance. Euclidean distance or simply 'distance' examines the root of square differences between coordinates of a pair of objects.
- Euclidian distance between two Objects A and Object B is given as follows:

$$d(A, B) = d(B, A) = \sqrt{(B_1 - A_1)^2 + (B_2 - A_2)^2 + ... + (B_n - A_n)^2} = \sqrt{\sum_{i=1}^{n} (B_i - A_i)^2}$$

- The Euclidean Distance between point A and B is,

$$d_{BA} = \sqrt{(0-7)^2 + (3-6)^2 + (4-3)^2 + (5+1)^2}$$
$$= \sqrt{49 + 9 + 1 + 36} = 9.747$$

- Euclidean distance is a special case of Minkowski distance with $\lambda = 2$.

City Block (Manhattan) Distance:

- It is also known as Manhattan distance, boxcar distance, absolute value distance. It examines the absolute differences between coordinates of a pair of objects.

$$d(A, B) = d(B, A) = \sqrt{|B_1 - A_1| + |B_2 - A_2| + ... + |B_3 - A_3|} = \sqrt{\sum_{i=1}^{n} |B_i - A_i|}$$

- The City Block Distance between point A and B is,

$$d_{BA} = |0 - 7| + |3 - 6| + |4 - 3| + |5 + 1|$$
$$= 7 + 3 + 1 + 6 = 17$$

Chebyshev Distance:

- Chebyshev distance is also called Maximum value distance. It examines the absolute magnitude of the differences between coordinates of a pair of objects.
- This distance can be used for both ordinal and quantitative variables,

$$d(A, B) = d(B, A) = \max_i |B_i - A_i|$$

- The Chebyshev Distance between point A and B is,

$$d_{BA} = \max \{|0 - 7|, |3 - 6|, |4 - 3|, |5 + 1|\}$$
$$= \max \{7, 3, 1, 6\} = 7$$

5.4.1 Requirement of Cluster Analysis

- Clustering is a fast growing and challenging research field. In this section, we will learn about the why clustering is required in data mining:
  1. **Scalability:** We need highly scalable clustering algorithms to deal with large databases. Clustering on only a sample of a given large data set may lead to biased results. Therefore, highly scalable clustering algorithms are needed.
  2. **Ability to deal with different kinds of Attributes:** Many algorithms are designed to cluster numeric (interval-based) data. However, applications may require clustering other data types, such as binary, nominal (categorical) and ordinal data or mixtures of these data types. Recently, more and more applications need clustering techniques for complex data types such as graphs, sequences, images, and documents.
  3. **Discovery of Clusters with Attribute Shape:** The clustering algorithm should be capable of detecting clusters of arbitrary shape. They should not be bounded to only distance measures that tend to find spherical cluster of small sizes.
  4. **High Dimensionality:** The clustering algorithm should not only be able to handle low-dimensional data but also the high dimensional space.
  5. **Ability to deal with Noisy Data:** Most real-world data sets contain outliers and/or missing, unknown, or erroneous data.. Some algorithms are sensitive to such data and may lead to poor quality clusters. Therefore, we need clustering methods that are robust to noise.
  6. **Interpretability and Usability**: The clustering results should be interpretable, comprehensible, and usable. i.e.; clustering may need to be tied in with specific semantic interpretations and applications. It is important to study how an application goal may influence the selection of clustering features and clustering methods.

5.5 OVERVIEW OF BASIC CLUSTERING METHODS

- There are various clustering techniques/algorithms in data mining organized into following categories:

Sr. No.	Clustering Methods	Explanation	Algorithms
1.	Partitioning Method	Partitioning based clustering algorithms divide the dataset into initial 'k' clusters and iteratively improve the clustering quality based on an objective function.	k-mean, Partitioning Around Medoids (PAM), CLARA, CLARANS, Expectation Maximization (EM).
2.	Hierarchical Method	Hierarchical clustering algorithms seek to build a hierarchy of cluster. They start with some initial clusters and gradually converge to the solution either in top-down or bottom-up approach.	Agglomerative hierarchical clustering, Divisive hierarchical clustering.
3.	Density Based Method	Density based clustering algorithms make an assumption that clusters are dense regions in space separated by regions of lower density. A dense cluster is a region which is "density connected", i.e. the density of points in that region is greater than a minimum. Since, these algorithms expand clusters based on dense connectivity, they can find clusters of arbitrary shapes.	DBSCAN.
4.	Grid Based Method	In grid based clustering algorithm, the entire dataset is overlaid by a regular hypergrid. The clusters are then formed by combining dense cells.	CLIQUE.

k-means Clustering Algorithm:

- k-means is one of the simplest unsupervised learning algorithms that solve the well-known clustering problem. The k-means algorithm partitions a given dataset into a user specified number of cluster 'k'.
- The procedure follows a simple and easy way to classify a given data set through a certain number of clusters (assume k clusters) fixed Apriori.
- The main idea is to define k centers, one for each cluster. These centers should be placed wisely so that of different location causes different result preferably place them as much as possible far away from each other.

- For example, the no of clusters you want to form is 3 then three center point you have to select one for each cluster.
- The next step is to take each point belonging to a given data set and associate it to the nearest center. When no point is pending, the first step is completed and an early group age is done.
- At this point we need to re-calculate k new centroids as barycenter of the clusters resulting from the previous step.
- After we have these k new centroids, a new binding has to be done between the same data set points and the nearest new center. A loop has been generated.
- As a result of this loop we may notice that the k centers change their location step by step until no more changes are done or in other words centers do not move any more.
- Finally, this algorithm aims at minimizing an objective function know as squared error function given by:

$$J(V) = \sum_{i=1}^{C} \sum_{j=1}^{C_i} (||x_i - v_j||)^2$$

where,

'$||x_i - v_j||$' is the Euclidean distance between x_i and v_j.

'c_i' is the number of data points in i^{th} cluster.

'c' is the number of cluster centers.

Algorithmic steps for k-means Clustering:

- The k-means algorithm for partitioning, where each cluster's center is represented by the mean value of the objects in the cluster.

Input:

k: The number of clusters,

D: A data set containing n objects.

Output: A set of k clusters.

Method:

1. Arbitrarily choose k objects from D as the initial cluster centres;
2. Repeat until no more reassignment/relaxation.

   (re)assign each object to the cluster to which the object is the most similar, based on the mean value of the objects in the cluster;

   update the cluster means, i.e., calculate the mean value of the objects for each cluster;

Advantages:

1. Fast, robust, easier to understand and easier to adapt.
2. Relatively efficient O(tknd), where n is # objects, k is # clusters, d is # dimension of each object, and t is # iterations. Normally, k, t, d << n.
3. Gives best result when data set are distinct or well separated from each other.
4. Simple to implement and run.

Disadvantages:

1. The learning algorithm requires specification of the number of cluster centers in prior.
2. The use of exclusive assignment - if there are two highly overlapping data then k-means will not be able to resolve that there are two clusters.
3. The learning algorithm is not invariant to non-linear transformations i.e. with different representation of data we get different results
4. Euclidean distance measures can unequally weight underlying factors.
5. The learning algorithm provides the local optima of the squared error function.

6. Randomly choosing of the cluster center cannot lead us to the fruitful result.
7. Applicable only when mean is defined i.e. fails for categorical data.
8. Unable to handle noisy data and outliers.
9. Algorithm fails for non-linear data set.

Example: Consider the following data set consisting of the scores of two variables on each of seven individuals:

Individual	A	B
1	1.0	1.0
2	1.5	2.0
3	3.0	4.0
4	5.0	7.0
5	3.5	5.0
6	4.5	5.0
7	3.5	4.5

- This data set is to be grouped into two clusters i.e. k=2.
- As a first step in finding a sensible initial partition, let the two individuals furthest apart (using the Euclidean distance measure), define the initial cluster means, giving:

	Individual	Mean Vector (Centroid)
Cluster1	1	(1.0, 1.0)
Cluster2	4	(5.0, 7.0)

- Compute the distance of each point of A, B corresponding to Centroid1 and Centroid2. The each individuals are now examined in sequence and allocated to the cluster to which they are closest, in terms of Euclidean distance to the cluster mean.

Subject	A	B	Distance from Centroid 1 (1.0, 1.0)	Distance from Centroid 2 (5.0, 7.0)	Select Minimum Distance	Cluster
1	1.0	1.0	0	7.2	0	1
2	1.5	2.0	1.11	6.10	1.11	1
3	3.0	4.0	3.60	3.6	3.6	1
4	5.0	7.0	7.2	0	0	2
5	3.5	5.0	4.71	2.5	2.5	2
6	4.5	5.0	5.3	2.06	2.06	2
7	3.5	4.5	4.30	2.91	2.91	2

Calculate the new centroid by calculating the mean of clusters. This leads to the following series of steps:

	Individuals	A	B	Mean Vector (Centroid)	
Cluster1	1	1.0	1.0	1.8	2.3
	2	1.5	2.0		
	3	3.0	4.0		
Cluster2	4	5.0	7.0	4.1	5.3
	5	3.5	5.0		
	6	4.5	5.0		
	7	3.5	4.5		

- Now the initial partition has changed, and the two clusters at this stage having the following characteristics:

	Individual	Mean Vector (centroid)
Cluster1	1, 2, 3	(1.8, 2.3)
Cluster2	4, 5, 6, 7	(4.1, 5.3)

- Compute the distance of each point of A, B corresponding to new Centroid1 and new centroid2. The each individuals are now examined in sequence and allocated to the cluster to which they are closest, in terms of Euclidean distance to the cluster mean.

Individual	A	B	Distance from new Centroid1 (1.8, 2.3)	Distance from new Centroid2 (4.1,5.3)	Select Minimum Distance	Cluster
1	1.0	1.0	1.57	5.30	1.57	1
2	1.5	2.0	0.42	4.20	0.42	1
3	3.0	4.0	2.08	1.70	1.70	2
4	5.0	7.0	5.64	1.92	1.92	2
5	3.5	5.0	3.19	0.67	0.67	2
6	4.5	5.0	3.81	0.5	0.5	2
7	3.5	4.5	2.78	1	1	2

- Only individual 3 is nearer to the mean of the opposite cluster (Cluster2) than its own (Cluster1). In other words, each individual's distance to its own cluster mean should be smaller that the distance to the other cluster's mean (which is not the case with individual 3).

	Individual	A	B	Mean Vector (Centroid)	
Cluster1	1	1.0	1.0	1.25	1.5
	2	1.5	2.0		
Cluster2	3	3.0	4.0	3.9	5.1
	4	5.0	7.0		
	5	3.5	5.0		
	6	4.5	5.0		
	7	3.5	4.5		

- Thus, individual 3 is relocated to Cluster2 resulting in the new partition:

	Individual	Mean Vector (Centroid)
Cluster1	1, 2	(1.25, 1.5)
Cluster2	3, 4, 5, 6, 7	(3.9, 5.1)

- The iterative relocation would now continue from this new partition until no more relocations occur.

5.6 GENERAL APPLICATIONS OF CLUSTERING

- Clustering analysis is broadly used in many applications such as market research, pattern recognition, data analysis, and image processing.
- Following are the possible area where clustering is used for research activity:
  1. Clustering can help in many fields such as in biology, plants, and animals classified by their properties. In biology, it is used for the determination of plant and animal taxonomies, for the categorization of genes with similar functionality and for insight into population-inherent structures.
  2. Clustering can also help marketers discover distinct groups in their customer base. And they can characterize their customer groups based on the purchasing patterns. Clustering can also help advertisers in their customer base to find different groups. And their customer groups can be defined by buying patterns.
  3. In an earth observation database, clustering also makes it easier to find areas of similar use in the land. It helps to identify groups of houses and apartments by type, value, and destination of houses. Clustering is also helpful in Earthquake studies where clustering observed earthquake epicenters to identify dangerous zones.
  4. Clustering is also used in outlier detection applications such as detection of credit card fraud, intrusion detection system.
  5. The clustering of documents on the web is also helpful for the discovery of information.
  6. Clustering is used in insurance companies for identifying groups of motor insurance policy holders with a high average claim cost; identifying frauds.
  7. Clustering is helpful in Astronomy where It helps to find groups of similar stars and galaxies.

Practice Questions

1. What is frequent pattern?
2. What is cluster?
3. Define the following items : (i) Clustering, (ii) Association Analysis.
4. How to mining frequent pattern? Explain with example.
5. What is market basket analysis. Explain with example.
6. Explain different association rule measures.
7. Explain frequent itemset and closed itemset with example.
8. Explain Arpiori algorithm with example.
9. Explain how to generate association rule from frequent itemset.
10. What is cluster analysis? Explain with example.
11. Explain different measures of similarity in clustering
12. Explain any one clustering approach in detail with example.
13. List applications of clustering.
14. Compare cluster analysis and association analysis.

✤ ✤ ✤